Mark McEwan

Mark McEwan
Great Food at Home

with Jacob Richler

VIKING
CANADA

VIKING CANADA

Published by the Penguin Group

Penguin Group (Canada), 90 Eglinton Avenue East, Suite 700, Toronto, Ontario, Canada M4P 2Y3
(a division of Pearson Canada Inc.)

Penguin Group (USA) Inc., 375 Hudson Street, New York, New York 10014, U.S.A.
Penguin Books Ltd, 80 Strand, London WC2R 0RL, England
Penguin Ireland, 25 St Stephen's Green, Dublin 2, Ireland (a division of Penguin Books Ltd)
Penguin Group (Australia), 250 Camberwell Road, Camberwell, Victoria 3124, Australia (a division
of Pearson Australia Group Pty Ltd)
Penguin Books India Pvt Ltd, 11 Community Centre, Panchsheel Park, New Delhi – 110 017, India
Penguin Group (NZ), 67 Apollo Drive, Rosedale, North Shore 0745, Auckland, New Zealand (a division
of Pearson New Zealand Ltd)
Penguin Books (South Africa) (Pty) Ltd, 24 Sturdee Avenue, Rosebank, Johannesburg 2196, South Africa

Penguin Books Ltd, Registered Offices: 80 Strand, London WC2R 0RL, England

First published 2010

1 2 3 4 5 6 7 8 9 10

Cover and interior design: Mary Opper
Cover photo: Nikki Leigh McKean

LIBRARY AND ARCHIVES CANADA CATALOGUING IN PUBLICATION

McEwan, Mark
        Great food at home / Mark McEwan.

Includes index.
ISBN 978-0-670-06456-4

        1. Cookery. 2. Entertaining. I. Title.

TX652.M3644 2010   641.5   C2010-902121-5

Visit the Penguin Group (Canada) website at **www.penguin.ca**

Special and corporate bulk purchase rates available; please see **www.penguin.ca/corporatesales** or call
1-800-810-3104, ext. 2477 or 2474

Contents

Introduction

This is my first cookbook. "Why now?" you might reasonably ask. It's been more than thirty years since I walked into the Regal Constellation Hotel—long gone, now—out near Toronto's Pearson Airport, applied for a job in the kitchen, and had the good fortune to fall under the guidance of a European-trained Swiss chef named Joseph Vonlanthan, who saw fit to mentor me. I promise that it didn't take the three decades since to come up with 100 good recipes for a cookbook. But it did take a lot of time and a professional journey to get to the right place and the right culinary philosophy, and to arrive at the sort of thinking that I believe is genuinely useful to share.

My cooking is different now than it was in the 1980s and '90s. I'm proud of the elegant plates I used to prepare at the Sutton Place Hotel, Pronto, North 44, and chefs' venues like James Beard House, but nowadays I prefer simpler fare. Even back then I would never have pretended that I ate at home the sort of food that I cooked at work. I don't want or expect you to either. Eating well but unpretentiously at home is what this book is all about.

There are plenty of cookbooks out there chock full of studio-lit culinary fashion shots attached to elaborate recipes that no one ever cooks, and I never wanted to add a book to that list. Even when I first started thinking about my own cookbook, I knew that I would feel like a failure if I dropped by a friend's house and saw my book open on the coffee table, with a photo spread on display. In my mind's eye my book's success would be measured instead by the time it spent on the kitchen counter, a badly creased binding, oil-splattered pages, and an abundance of bookmarks and margin notes.

I had books like that, books I trusted, back when I was learning to cook. And what I set out to do here with my chefs and other collaborators was to create a volume like that, something for the catalogue of the well thumbed—a book home cooks would look to all the time, a book full of recipes for any occasion, a book they could count on for guidance on how to make anything from the simplest chicken stock to the most exotic risotto.

On that note, the range of recipes included here is substantial. Basics aside, a lot of the recipes reflect the sort of simple, rustic fare that I like to toss up at the cottage, from a mid-summer's plate of seared perch fillets with charred tomato risotto to a wintertime venison stew with mashed potatoes for eating fireside after a day's skiing. These are the sorts of things that I hope you will enjoy family-style, sharing them out unceremoniously from big serving plates at the table.

Other dishes were plucked directly from our restaurant menus at North 44, Bymark, and One, simplified some for the home cook, but nonetheless more appropriate to the sophisticated dinner party than a casual night in the countryside. I've included some of these for two reasons. First, it's natural to want to squeeze a bit of everything into your first book. And second, there were favourites from the restaurants over the years that I just had to include. To be frank, I didn't want anyone interrupting me at the bar at One to say, "How the hell could you put out a cookbook without including the halibut with the banana leaf?"

Whatever you choose to cook from these pages, and from whichever end of the spectrum of difficulty, I have the same few words of advice for you. First of all, be assured that all these recipes work as written, and work well—but all the same, your stove and your pans and your olive oil are all different from mine, so do keep in mind that even a well-written recipe is no substitute for experience and only the foolhardy cook tries out a new recipe for the first time for a dinner party.

Something else: always remember that good cooking is not a paint-by-numbers activity. When a food critic writes of a chef that his cooking has "passion" or "soul," the compliment means this: Chef made it up as he went along—and what great instincts! You should never be afraid to exchange one ingredient for another, or use a little less of one thing and a little more of something else, according to your taste, what looks best at the market, and what you find in the fridge when it's snowing out and you don't want to trudge to the store. You should relax and have fun with it.

All the same, there are a small number of basic rules to keep in mind when working through the recipes in this book. To begin, the simplest. Despite any appearances to the contrary, we did try to keep our lists of ingredients concise. With a view to that, when you see a request for "white wine" it means dry white wine, unless otherwise stated. The same goes for red wine. Unless the recipe states otherwise, "pepper" is freshly ground black pepper, "flour" means all-purpose flour, "butter" is unsalted, and herbs are fresh. Where pasta is called for, you may use dry or fresh. For an appetizer portion, count on 2 oz (60 g) dry or 3 oz (90 g) fresh per person; for a main course serving, use 3½ oz (100 g) dry or 5 oz (150 g) fresh.

As for oils, when a recipe calls for "olive oil" it means a most basic one, because anything better is wasted in the sauté pan. Top-quality extra virgin olive oil has too much flavour for that role and also burns easily. It is to be used instead for finishing a dish—seasoning it after it has been cooked. When a recipe calls for that, it reads "fine olive oil." On the deep-frying front, in our restaurants we always use canola oil, but if you prefer the flavour and qualities of peanut oil, by all means use that instead.

We cook exclusively with kosher salt at our restaurants and respectfully recommend that you do the same, as it is mild and exceptionally versatile in the kitchen. Its mildness, however, also made it clear to us that our salt measurements would never translate exactly to whatever salt you might use in your kitchen. So we have provided measurements only for pastry, brines, and those other rare instances where instinct has no role. The rest of the time we decided on the guidelines "season lightly" and "season generously" and left the rest to you, for after all, preference in seasoning is personal. There is only one rule about salt that you must always follow: never, ever cook with iodized table salt, for its intense nature makes it completely inappropriate for the subtle task of seasoning while cooking.

The one other issue on which we hope to successfully petition the home cook is this: the best ingredients are always worth seeking out. Your results depend on it. Pallid factory chickens raised beakless in a fluorescent-lit barn are not the thing to showcase in our recipe for rustic roast chicken. If you make our risotto with bacon and peas with pre-sliced chemical-flooded industrial bacon instead of a hand-sliced piece from an old-school smokehouse, you will save $2 but end up wondering why you wasted those thirty minutes stirring the pot. And so on.

We encourage you to make your own stocks. If you lack the time or will, never use as a substitute a bouillon cube or something powdered, for the result will be abysmal in flavour and in texture. You can buy pre-made stocks, but choose carefully, and keep in mind that they tend to be thinly flavoured. My recipes for braises and the like do not call for bouquets garnis or sachets of dry spices because the stocks prepared from the recipes in the back of this book—which we use at our restaurants and sell at McEwan Fine Foods—are sufficiently full-flavoured on their own. If you use a lesser stock, you may want to add the herbs.

On which note, never consider these recipes to be rigid sets of instructions. Think of them instead as guidelines to be freely adapted according to taste and circumstance. Do not be afraid to change things when you do not have everything in a given list of ingredients. The recipe for halibut baked in a banana leaf has twenty-one flavourings. But there is no chemical formula in play that will collapse if you take one away; the recipe will still yield a very tasty piece of fish. When you are changing things up, just remember to think about the role of the ingredient in question and replace it with something similar. If, for example, a recipe calls for a little of one of our restaurant pantry staples like jalapeño paste and you quite reasonably do not want to make up a batch only to get the single teaspoon required, by all means chop up another hot pepper you have on hand and add that instead, or even a few drops of hot sauce.

Flexibility is the key to good cooking, and in this book we have tried to encourage that every way we know. For starters, many recipes include suggested alternatives to some of the principal ingredients. And rather than steer you towards strictly assembled plates, for each main course dish we have suggested whole ranges of complementary side dishes to choose from. You, after all, are the diner as well as the cook, and so it falls to you to decide what you like best.

I sincerely hope you enjoy cooking from the book as much as my chefs and I did putting it together.

Passed Appetizers

These dishes are in some ways the most versatile in the book, for they can all serve as anything from a casual snack to being passed around like canapés at an elegant cocktail party to being plated as a first course at a sit-down dinner.

Whether they require a lot of time and effort for their preparation or not very much at all, they all reveal the same truth in the end: you can fit an amazing amount of flavour, texture, and finesse into the smallest of packages.

Oxtail Empanadas

Swapping the firm shell of a traditional empanada for flaky French pastry, and abandoning its typical stuffings of potato, chorizo, or hot pepper for a refined, slow-braised oxtail ragù, is not an exercise in authenticity. But that hardly matters when it makes such good culinary sense. These little snacks are sublime. MAKES 30 EMPANADAS

2 sheets quick puff pastry (page 243) or
    frozen puff pastry, about 1 lb (450 g) total
Pinch each of salt and pepper
1 half-batch braised oxtail (page 228),
    no warmer than room temperature
1 egg, lightly beaten

Preheat oven to 425°F (220°C).

Flour a work surface and roll out each sheet of puff pastry to a 12-by-15-inch (30 by 38 cm) rectangle. Dust lightly with flour and a little salt and pepper. Cut each sheet lengthwise into three strips about 4 inches (10 cm) wide. Working with a 1-inch (2.5 cm) melon baller, place scoops of the oxtail mixture on the pastry, spacing the balls evenly along a row running the length of the strip and to one side of its centre line. Brush the other side of the strip with some of the egg wash and fold it over the oxtail balls. Using the dull edge of a knife, press the pastry together tightly all around the balls, working outwards from the hinge. Then cut the strip into individual triangular packages. Trim any excess pastry and then arrange the parcels on a baking sheet lined with parchment paper. Repeat to make 30 empanadas in all. Brush the empanadas with an egg wash and bake until golden brown—about 15 minutes.

Tip: If you are not going to bake the empanadas immediately after they are formed, they should be frozen, egg wash and all. They can go straight into the oven from the freezer; cooking time will be slightly longer, but not much.

Suggested wine: Côtes du Rhône or Rioja

Sweet Pea Crostini with Poached Egg

The pleasures of toast are rooted in childhood. Using the finest baguette, giving it a topping, and turning it into crostini renders it adult, at least outwardly. This version was conceived as a showcase for the first sweet peas of early summer. MAKES 12 CROSTINI

½ baguette, sliced diagonally, thickness to taste
3 tbsp (45 mL) olive oil
Salt
2 cups (500 mL) fresh sweet peas
2 tbsp (30 mL) minced mint
2 tbsp (30 mL) lemon juice
Pepper
4 eggs
1 tbsp (15 mL) warm milk
1 tbsp (15 mL) butter, melted
½ cup (125 mL) grated Parmigiano-Reggiano

Preheat the broiler. Sprinkle the baguette slices with 1 tbsp (15 mL) of the olive oil and some salt, then broil on both sides until golden. Set aside to cool.

Blanch the peas in boiling salted water until tender, about 2 minutes. Shock in ice water and drain well. Chop the peas, and combine them in a bowl with the mint, lemon juice and remaining 2 tbsp (30 mL) olive oil and mix well (or blitz whole peas very briefly with the other ingredients in a food processor). Season and set aside.

Poach the eggs until soft, about 3 minutes. Drain on paper towels, then transfer to a bowl. Chop the eggs with the edge of a spoon. Stir in the milk and butter, and adjust seasonings.

Spread the pea mixture on the toasts and follow with a little of the egg mixture. Top with a sprinkle of Parmesan.

Substitutions: For a more refined presentation, top each crostini with a whole poached quail egg in place of the chopped egg.

Tip: If fresh peas are not in season, you are better off using frozen ones (plunged briefly into boiling salted water, refreshed in ice water, and drained) rather than some once fresh and now jet-lagged edition from the "fresh" produce section of the supermarket.

Suggested wine: Sancerre or other crisp Sauvignon Blanc

Lobster Tacos

Like Mexico's finest fish tacos, these burst with vibrant flavour on the palate, and run the gamut of textures, too. The beet taco shell is our own touch that brings a splendid colour to the package. While slightly time-consuming to prepare, these tacos are well worth the effort, perfect for passing around at a cocktail party or as a first course. MAKES 12 SMALL TACOS

1 live lobster, about 1¼ lb (625 g)
1 large red beet
Oil for deep-frying
Flour for dredging
1 jicama, peeled
1 lime
3 tbsp (45 mL) lemon-garlic aïoli (page 223)

Pinch each of salt and pepper
2 tsp (10 mL) finely chopped chives
12 slices Japanese-style pickled ginger
6 cilantro leaves, halved
¼ cup (50 mL) julienned leek greens (optional)
Fragrant soy (optional; page 234)

Bring a large pot of salted water to a vigorous boil, plunge the lobster into the pot head first, cover, reduce heat, and simmer for 10 minutes. Remove lobster, cool under cold running water, and drain. Shell the lobster, and set meat aside in the refrigerator.

Cut the beet in half crosswise and then, with the aid of a mandoline, slice off 10 or so paper-thin discs from each half. Using a 2- to 2½-inch (5 to 6 cm) circular cutter—or an inverted small drinking glass and a sharp pointed knife—cut the beet discs into identical rounds.

Heat deep-fryer—or oil in a deep skillet—to 400°F (200°C). Dredge the beet slices lightly in flour and shake off excess. Then drop them in small batches into the hot oil and use a spider or slotted spoon to submerge them completely. When after 40 to 60 seconds the bubbling subsides—meaning that the water has evaporated from inside the beets—transfer the beets in a single row to a bed of paper towels. Place another row of paper towels on top, then align a 1-inch (2.5 cm) diameter pipe (or a broomstick handle wrapped in foil) over the row of beet discs and wrap the package tightly around the cylinder. After 30 seconds the beets will have set; remove the hard taco shells to a fresh paper towel. (The shells can be made the day before, but must be stored in an airtight container as they will quickly lose their crispness in the open air.)

Trim the jicama so that it sits squarely on the chopping board, and then cut from it a broad slice no thicker than ⅛ inch (3 mm). Then slice that into 2½-inch (6 cm) long batonets. Repeat if needed until you have at least 36 batonets. Cut the lime in half crosswise, and then take a ⅛-inch (3 mm) slice from each half. With a small knife, cut at least 12 triangular segments of lime from their coarse surrounding membrane and set aside. Juice the remaining halves. Dice the reserved lobster, and in a bowl toss with the aïoli. Adjust seasoning, add the chives and lime juice to taste, and toss again.

To avoid soggy shells, assemble the tacos immediately before serving. Select the best 12 shells. In the bottom of each, place lengthwise two or three batonets of jicama, followed by a slice of pickled ginger. Using a fork—so as to not add too much liquid—add a scoop of lobster. Garnish each taco with a lime segment and a cilantro leaf.

Create a topple-resistant serving plate by scattering it with julienned leek or dressing it with a folded cloth napkin, and place tacos carefully on top. Serve with fragrant soy for dipping, if desired.

Suggested wine: Viognier

Lobster Spoons

Lobster meat toughens rapidly when it's overheated or overcooked. If the meat is instead cooked gently, it will be soft, supple, and tender. There is no better way to achieve this result than by removing the lobster meat from its shell when virtually raw and then poaching it slowly in *beurre monté*. **Presenting the lobster in spoons containing a single mouthful showcases the trick unadorned as an exquisite hors d'oeuvre. MAKES 12 SPOONS**

1 live lobster, about 1½ lb (750 g), par-cooked and shelled (page 237)
Pinch each of salt and pepper

BEURRE MONTÉ
2 tbsp (30 mL) dry vermouth
1 lb (450 g) cold butter, cubed

GARNISH
Leaves from 1 sprig cilantro, halved or roughly chopped

BEURRE MONTÉ: Over medium heat, heat the vermouth in a medium saucepan until it begins to bubble, and then lower heat. Add a piece of butter and whisk until it emulsifies. Continue adding butter, a piece at a time, until all the butter is incorporated. Keep warm at a temperature between 160 and 180°F (70 and 85°C) to preserve the emulsion.

Cut the lobster into small bite-size pieces. Add to the beurre monté and cook until heated through—3 to 4 minutes. Season.

Arrange 12 Chinese white porcelain soup spoons on a platter or two. Dress each spoon with a pinch of cilantro, then divide lobster evenly among the spoons. Drizzle a little extra *beurre monté* on top, and serve.

Suggested wine: buttery Chardonnay

Mini Crab Falafels

The chefs at Bymark enjoy a preoccupation with elevating common snacks to something above their station. In this version of the Middle Eastern roadside falafel, the chickpea is banished for a more delicate combination of fava bean and sweet pea, and for the *coup de grâce*, the well-seasoned mixture is larded with crabmeat. Not kosher and hardly halal—but delicious all the same. MAKES 20 MINI FALAFELS

2 cups (500 mL) shelled fava beans, blanched and peeled
½ cup (125 mL) sweet peas, blanched
¼ cup (50 mL) minced parsley
¼ cup (50 mL) minced dill
¼ cup (50 mL) minced cilantro
3 scallions, greens only, minced
4 oz (125 g) cooked crabmeat, picked over
½ tsp (2 mL) cumin seeds, toasted and ground
½ tsp (2 mL) coriander seeds, toasted and ground
¼ tsp (1 mL) chili flakes
Salt and pepper
½ cup (125 mL) clarified butter
½ cup (125 mL) canola or vegetable oil

Flour for dredging
2 eggs, lightly beaten
2 cups (500 mL) panko bread crumbs

TABBOULEH
2 Roma tomatoes, diced
¼ English cucumber, seeded and diced
1 cup (250 mL) chopped Italian parsley
½ cup (125 mL) diced red onion
2 tbsp (30 mL) lemon juice
Pinch each of salt and pepper
1 bag of mini pita breads
1 cup (250 mL) lemon-garlic aïoli (page 223)

Combine the fava beans, sweet peas, parsley, dill, cilantro, and scallions in a food processor and pulse in very short bursts about six times until combined but not smooth—the mixture must remain textured. In a bowl, combine the crab, cumin, coriander, and chili flakes; toss well. Add fava mixture to crab mixture; season and mix well. Form into about 20 small pucks and arrange in a single layer on a baking sheet lined with parchment paper. Chill for at least 30 minutes.

MEANWHILE, MAKE TABBOULEH: Combine the tomatoes, cucumber, parsley, onion, and lemon juice in a bowl, season, and toss well. Set aside.

Begin heating the butter and oil in a large skillet to frying temperature—about 350°F (180°C). Working in small batches to avoid a crowded pan or soggy crust, dredge the patties first in the flour, then in the eggs, and finally in the panko. Fry them one batch at a time until golden and crisp on both sides. Transfer to paper towels to drain.

Cut mini pitas in half, insert a falafel into each pocket, adorn the protruding falafel with a dab of lemon-garlic aïoli, and finish with a small mound of tabbouleh.

Suggested wine: Alsatian Pinot Gris

Soups

Linguistically speaking, it must be said that we do not give soup its proper due. The French, from whom we learned a thing or two in the kitchen, have an entire vocabulary built around the notion: not just *la soupe* but *purée, bisque, velouté, crème, potage,* and *consommé,* each denoting a distinct interpretation of a liquid-based meal in bowl. *La soupe* is so important to the French that it can be taken to mean food itself. *Je vie de bonne soupe et non de beau langage,* Molière wrote—"It's good food and not fine words that keeps me alive."

Fortunately our culinary vocabulary does not tie our hands in the kitchen, and we have made up for it here with a wide range of styles and ingredients. You will find a soup for occasions casual and formal, and weather cold and hot. And of course we have included the definitive chowder, our only other word for soup—for which we owe the French Canadians and their distinctive cooking pot, *la chaudière.*

Corn Bisque with Foie Gras Crostini

This sweet purée delivers one of the most memorable and evocative flavours of the Canadian summer in an elegant form that spares you the customary indignities of tooth trouble and butter on the chin. And the foie gras–smeared crostini makes it all add up to something much more than the sum of its parts. SERVES 6

8 ears of sweet corn in their husks
¼ cup (50 mL) olive oil
1 medium Spanish onion, chopped
4 cloves garlic, chopped
2 red bell peppers—1 chopped, 1 diced
2 green bell peppers—1 chopped, 1 diced
1 large sweet potato—¾ chopped, ¼ diced
1 cup (250 mL) white wine
Salt and pepper
1 quart (1 L) white chicken stock (page 246)
4 oz (125 g) foie gras mousse, at room temperature
6 slices (5 in/12 cm long) baguette, toasted
1 tsp (5 mL) truffle oil (optional)

Grill or roast the whole ears of corn until the kernels are just cooked—10 to 12 minutes. Shuck them. Slice off the kernels, and reserve. Hack the cobs into six or seven pieces each. Heat 2 to 3 tbsp (30 to 45 mL) of the oil in a large saucepan over medium heat, and sauté the onions, garlic, and corn cobs for 2 or 3 minutes. Add the chopped bell pepper and chopped sweet potato along with three-quarters of the corn kernels. (Set aside the remaining corn.) Cook, stirring occasionally, until the vegetables are soft, then deglaze the pot with the wine. Season lightly, add the chicken stock, and simmer, uncovered, for 30 minutes.

Discard the corn cob pieces. Working in batches, purée the soup in a blender until smooth. Transfer to a clean pot.

Blanch the diced bell pepper in boiling salted water for 45 to 60 seconds, then shock in ice water and drain. Do the same with the diced sweet potato.

When ready to serve, reheat the bisque. Spread the foie gras mousse on the toasts. In the remaining olive oil, quickly sauté the blanched red pepper and sweet potato along with reserved corn. Pour the hot bisque into warm bowls, place a generous spoonful of the sautéed vegetables in the centre, and then gently place a foie gras crostini as a bridge from the edge of the bowl to the island of vegetables in the soup. If you choose, finish with a small drizzle of truffle oil.

Variation: In place of the crostini, top each mound of vegetables with a generous morsel of butter-poached lobster (page 131).

Golden Gazpacho

The origins of gazpacho as we know it date to the mid-eighteenth century, and the intervening years have been marked by one assault after another on its supremacy as the most refreshing, invigorating, and nutritious of summer soups. But none has succeeded in knocking it off its pedestal, not even for a year or two. Our variation on this classic features yellow tomatoes instead of red, and some jicama to enhance its crunch. SERVES 8

5 lb (2.2 kg) ripe yellow tomatoes
½ English cucumber, peeled
½ small yellow zucchini, finely diced
½ small green zucchini, finely diced
1 red bell pepper, finely diced
1 yellow bell pepper, finely diced
¼ jicama, peeled and finely diced
½ red onion, finely diced
¼ bunch cilantro, minced
½ cup (125 mL) white wine vinegar
½ tsp (2 mL) Worcestershire sauce—or more to taste
¼ tsp (1 mL) Tabasco—or more to taste
2 tbsp (30 mL) olive oil
Salt and pepper
Chive oil (page 232) or fine olive oil
Fleur de sel

Blitz tomatoes in a food processor and then pass them through a sieve into a large bowl. Do the same with the cucumber. Add the green and yellow zucchini, red and yellow bell peppers, jicama, onion, cilantro, vinegar, Worcestershire, Tabasco, and olive oil. Stir well. To improve its texture, pulse the soup for two short bursts in a blender—or do so for slightly longer with a hand wand. Season, then cover and chill overnight. Before serving, sprinkle soup lightly with chive oil and a pinch of fleur de sel.

Variations: Simply exchange the yellow tomatoes for red ones to make a more traditional gazpacho. To enrich the soup, enhance it with garlic croutons (page 234) or non-vegetarian additions such as diced cooked lobster (page 237) or shrimp, or crumbled smoked black cod.

Roasted Tomato Soup with Basil Mousse

The culinary marriage of tomato and basil is one of a small handful that simply cannot be improved upon. With this soup we enrich the union by intensifying the tomato flavour by combining roasted tomatoes with stewed ones, as well as enlivening the basil with cream. The result is a rich purée with great purity of flavour. SERVES 6

12 Roma tomatoes, halved, cored,
    and seeded
4 tbsp (60 mL) fine olive oil
Pinch each of salt and pepper
Leaves from 2 sprigs basil
1 large Spanish onion, sliced
2 cloves garlic, crushed
1 tbsp (15 mL) toasted fennel seeds

1 cup (250 mL) white wine
2 cups (500 mL) top-quality canned Italian
    Roma tomatoes, juice included
2 cups (500 mL) vegetable stock

BASIL MOUSSE
½ cup (125 mL) loosely packed basil leaves
½ cup (125 mL) 35% cream

Preheat oven to 450°F (230°C).

Spread the tomatoes on a baking sheet large enough to accommodate them in a single layer. Sprinkle with half the olive oil, season generously with salt and pepper, and then toss so that they are evenly coated. Arrange them cut side down, scatter with half the basil leaves, and then roast for approximately 15 minutes—or until their skins begin to char and blister. Set aside.

Heat a large saucepan over medium-high heat and sauté the onions and garlic in the remaining olive oil. After 5 minutes add the fennel seeds. When the onions begin to turn colour, lower the heat. Continue to stir regularly until the onions are thoroughly bronzed, then raise heat to medium-high and deglaze the pan with the wine.

Add to the pot the roasted tomatoes (unpeeled) and basil, the canned tomatoes with their juice, and the stock. Stir well, bring to a gentle simmer, and then once again lower the heat. Season with salt and pepper to taste. Add the remaining basil leaves and simmer, uncovered, for no more than 30 minutes. In batches if necessary, whiz the soup in a blender until smooth, then pass through a fine-mesh sieve.

BASIL MOUSSE: Blanch the basil leaves for 30 seconds and shock in ice water. Drain and squeeze dry in a paper towel. Chop very finely. Whip the cream and the basil in a bowl until the cream forms firm peaks. Refrigerate until ready to serve.

To serve, return the soup to a simmer, adjust seasoning, and top each serving with a single quenelle of basil mousse.

Substitutions: To attain an even richer tomato flavour, replace the vegetable stock with an equal amount of tomato water (page 249). For a lighter soup, cold water may be used instead of the stock.

Tip: Fennel seeds burn easily, so rather than toasting them in a dry skillet, spread them evenly on a cookie sheet and roast them for 5 minutes in an oven preheated to 325°F (160°C).

New England Clam Chowder

Most Canadian Maritime chowders rely on milk for enrichment, while New England chowders always use cream—and typically flour, too, as a thickening agent. Ours instead builds body from the cream itself, which we reduce until it is as thick as Devon cream. Then we lighten the rich result with lemon juice. SERVES 4

1 quart (1 L) 35% cream
¼ cup (50 mL) grapeseed or canola oil
½ medium carrot, diced
1 cup (250 mL) diced onion
1 cup (250 mL) diced celery
4 bay leaves
½ bunch thyme
5 lb (2.2 kg) littleneck or Manila clams, scrubbed

¼ cup (50 mL) white wine
1 bottle (8 oz/250 mL) clam juice
1 quart (1 L) fish stock (page 246)
¼ lb (125 g) good-quality bacon, chopped
1 large russet potato, about 1 lb (450 g), peeled and diced
1 tbsp (15 mL) minced parsley
1 tsp (5 mL) lemon juice
Salt and pepper

Simmer the cream over low heat until reduced by half; set aside. In a large sauté pan, heat half the oil over medium-low heat and briefly sweat the carrot and about ¼ cup (50 mL) each of the onion and celery. Add 1 bay leaf and 3 sprigs of thyme. Turn up the heat and add the clams. Splash in the wine, ½ cup (125 mL) of the clam juice, and the fish stock, then cover the pot. When the liquid begins to boil, lower the heat to a simmer. Remove the clams as they pop open, and set aside. (Discard any clams that don't open.)

In a saucepan heat the remaining oil over medium-low heat and cook the bacon until it starts to brown slightly at the edges. Discard excess fat, and then add the remaining onion, celery, and bay leaves. Do not let brown. When the vegetables soften, add the potatoes and cook, stirring, for a minute or two. Strip leaves from the remaining thyme, mince, and add 1 tbsp (15 mL) to the soup. Add the remaining clam juice. Strain the clam poaching liquid through a fine-mesh sieve set over the pot. Strain the reduced cream through the sieve into the pot. Simmer until the potatoes are just beginning to soften. Then add the clams, parsley, and lemon juice, stir well, and adjust seasonings.

Chicken Noodle Soup

We are saddled with many a culinary cliché that, while now tired and tasteless, once sprouted from a very sound idea. And there is probably no better example of good culinary thinking collapsing under the collective abuse of bad diners and the dusty tinned-soup section of your local supermarket than chicken noodle soup. Our best-ingredients-only restoration went on the menu at One on opening day—and popular demand has kept it there ever since. SERVES 4

1 celery stalk, sliced
1 large carrot, peeled, halved lengthwise, and sliced
8 pearl onions, unpeeled
¼ lb (125 g) dry pasta of choice
2 quarts (2 L) white or dark chicken stock (page 246)
½ roast chicken (page 172), skinned, and shredded (about 2 cups/500 mL)
Pinch each of salt and pepper
1 tbsp (15 mL) chopped parsley

Blanch the celery until just tender and then shock in ice water. Drain. Repeat with the carrot. Blanch the pearl onions until soft and shock in ice water; trim off the root end and then squeeze hard between thumb and forefinger so that the separate layers of onion pop out the bottom. Cook the pasta, drain, and shock in cold water to stop the cooking.

In a large pot, bring the stock to a boil. Add the chicken and vegetables and heat through. Correct seasonings. Add the pasta, ladle the soup into warm bowls, and sprinkle with parsley.

Tip: This is a great dish for using up leftovers, not just of the roast chicken itself but also the carcasses from roast chickens past, which you can store in the freezer and use for making the stock.

Seafood Consommé

This light take on bouillabaisse is well equipped with vibrant flavour but manages without the richness of saffron. That and the delicacy of its lightly cooked seafood make it an ideal fish soup for summertime. Vary the seafood according to what looks best at the market. SERVES 4

2 skinless white fish fillets (sea bass, Atlantic cod,
    halibut, or the like), about 6 oz (175 g) each
12 large shrimp, shelled and deveined
6 dry-packed sea scallops
1 yellow onion, chopped
½ leek, white part only, chopped
1 celery stalk, chopped
6 egg whites, beaten to a froth
10 cups (2.5 L) cold fish stock (page 246)
5 sprigs thyme
1 bay leaf
Salt and white pepper

OPTIONAL GARNISH
Chervil leaves

Pass 1 fish fillet, 4 shrimp, and 2 scallops through a meat grinder equipped with a coarse blade—or whiz very briefly in a food processor. Combine in a bowl with onion, leek, and celery. Fold in the frothed egg whites. Transfer to a pot and add the cold stock, thyme, and bay leaf. Stir well and heat on medium until it begins to simmer, stirring regularly the whole time, but stopping as soon as the soup begins to bubble and the "raft" begins to form. Poke a few holes in its surface with the handle of a wooden spoon, and then do not disturb it again, leaving the broth to simmer until the liquid bubbling through the holes no longer appears cloudy—45 to 60 minutes. Strain the consommé through a sieve lined with cheesecloth into a clean pot.

Reheat the consommé, taste, and adjust seasonings. Slice the remaining fish fillet into thin bite-size pieces. Slice each scallop into 4 or 5 discs. Cut the shrimp into bite-size morsels. Place the raw seafood in the bottom of a warm soup tureen or individual bowls, pour the hot consommé over it, garnish with chervil, and serve.

Garlic Soup with Shredded Duck Confit and Pastry Dome

In 1975, when the incomparable Chef Paul Bocuse was awarded the Cross of the *Légion d'honneur* as Ambassador of French cooking, he commemorated the occasion with a freshly invented first course: a rich consommé served under a pastry dome. Each bowl featured a slice of foie gras and nearly two ounces of truffle. Our take is almost as rich, and a whole lot more affordable. SERVES 4

2 tbsp (30 mL) duck fat
½ Spanish onion, chopped
3 heads of roasted garlic (page 243), squeezed
2 tsp (10 mL) minced thyme
½ cup (125 mL) white wine
6 cups (1.5 L) white chicken stock (page 246)
2 tbsp (30 mL) grated Parmigiano-Reggiano
Salt and white pepper
2 confit duck legs (page 231), warmed, skin removed
    and meat shredded
1 sheet puff pastry, about ½ lb (250 g) total
1 egg, lightly beaten

Preheat oven to 400°F (200°C).

In a heavy-bottomed pot, melt the duck fat over medium-low heat and sweat the onion until it wilts. Add the garlic and thyme and then deglaze with the wine. When the wine has all but evaporated, add the stock. Bring to a boil and simmer, uncovered, for 30 minutes. Purée the soup in a blender until smooth and pass it through a fine-mesh sieve into a clean pot. Reheat, add the cheese, and adjust seasonings—but under-salt in deference to the Parmesan and the duck, which are both salty on their own.

Divide the confit among four ovenproof bowls, then do the same with the soup. Roll the pastry out to a thickness of about ⅛ inch (3 mm) and then cut it into discs about 1 inch (2.5 cm) wider than the soup bowls. Brush the perimeter of the pastry with egg wash, then drape it over the soup bowl egg wash side down, pressing lightly against the bowl all around to make a seal. Brush top of pastry with remaining egg wash and transfer bowls to the hot oven. Bake until pastry puffs up into a bronzed dome—10 to 15 minutes.

Substitutions: This rich, garlicky velouté will serve as a lovely backdrop for any number of different meats and fowl. Try the soup with leftover turkey or some shredded short rib.

Tip: Even store-bought duck confit should come packaged with enough duck fat to use for sautéing the onions. If not, use olive oil instead.

Cauliflower Bisque with Seared Sea Scallop and Crispy Sage

There is a minor alchemy at play here, in that while this cauliflower purée tastes rich and buttery, there is in fact no butter in the mix—nor even any cream. The soup is a perfect backdrop for innumerable additions. We do it with scallops, with foie gras, and with shredded duck confit and parsnip. By all means try your own. SERVES 8

BISQUE
1 head of cauliflower, about 2 lb (1 kg), sliced
2½ quarts (2.5 L) milk
Salt and white pepper
Pinch of nutmeg

SCALLOPS
8 dry-packed sea scallops
Salt
1½ tbsp (23 mL) butter
1 tsp (5 mL) olive oil

GARNISH
1 tbsp (15 mL) chive oil (page 232)
16 crispy sage leaves (page 180), crumbled

Combine cauliflower and milk in a pot, season lightly, and bring to a simmer over medium-low heat, stirring frequently to ensure that the milk does not burn. Simmer, stirring regularly, for about an hour—or until the cauliflower falls apart when pierced with a fork. Pour off 3 cups (750 mL) of the milk, strain and reserve. Purée the remaining cauliflower and milk in a blender, in batches if necessary, then pass it through a fine-mesh sieve into a clean pot. Bring soup to a simmer. Adjust the consistency by adding some of the reserved milk. Correct the seasonings. Keep warm.

Preheat oven to 450°F (230°C).

Pat scallops dry and salt them generously. Thoroughly heat an ovenproof nonstick skillet over medium-high, then sear the scallops. When they appear bronzed at the base—after 2 or 3 minutes—add the butter and oil, turn the scallops, and transfer the skillet to the oven. Cook for 6 or 7 minutes or until medium-rare and well bronzed on both sides. Remove scallops to the cutting board and slice each in half crosswise. Leave one half of each scallop intact and cut the remaining halves into 4 or 5 pieces each.

Pour the soup into serving bowls. Cluster two or three scallop pieces in the middle of each. Place a scallop half, bronzed side up, on top, and add a few more scallop pieces around the edges. Garnish with a drizzle of chive oil and a scattering of crumbled crispy sage.

Substitutions: The cauliflower purée is a versatile flavour base. Instead of scallops you may use roughly chopped seared foie gras (allow 1 oz/30 g per serving) combined with an equal amount of caramelized parsnip, or shredded duck confit with its crispy skin on top, or cubed lobster meat (allow 2 oz /60 g of either per serving). Each alternative is equally complemented by the chive oil and sage.

Tip: Do not worry about overcooking the cauliflower—but do avoid undercooking it, or the soup will taste gritty.

Salads

These seven salads will enhance your repertoire well beyond what their number might suggest. Some can make up a casual summer lunch all on their own. Others make a fine first course at a dinner party. Some can be largely made ahead and finished off quickly to impressive effect after the guests have arrived. Two of them require genuine finesse in the kitchen—but to offset that we added another that can be tossed up in under a minute, and requires only a quick wipe of the chopping block for cleanup.

What they all have in common is a certain simplicity. In contrast to the emperor's complaint to Mozart in *Amadeus*, none of them has "too many notes." The flavours and textures of their constituent parts are distinct in the mix. And that's the way things should be, especially when a good number of your ingredients are raw. The trick of it is to use the best ones you can find.

Fingerling Potatoes and French Green Beans with Classic Vinaigrette

Potatoes, green beans, and vinaigrette make for a classic combination that is considerably enhanced when the potato in the mix is a firm, nutty fingerling and the green beans are of the slender, delicate French variety. We go one step further by including some perfectly seared scallops, in which guise the salad works best warm—but if you omit the seafood you may serve it cold to equally pleasing effect. SERVES 4

16 fingerling potatoes, about 1 lb (450 g) total, scrubbed
1½ lb (750 g) French green beans
⅓ cup (75 mL) white wine vinegar
1 tbsp (15 mL) freshly grated horseradish
1 tsp (5 mL) Dijon mustard
⅔ cup (150 mL) olive oil

Salt and pepper
Leaves from 2 large sprigs Italian parsley, chopped
8 dry-packed sea scallops
1½ tbsp (23 mL) butter
1 tsp (5 mL) olive oil

Preheat oven to 450°F (230°C).

Boil potatoes in salted water until fork-tender—15 to 20 minutes. Remove from water and set aside. Blanch beans for 2 minutes, then shock in ice water. Combine the vinegar, horseradish, mustard, oil, and a pinch of salt and pepper in a bowl and whisk together thoroughly. Add half the parsley. Set aside half the dressing. Slice the potatoes in half lengthwise and add to the bowl along with the green beans; toss well. Adjust seasonings.

Meanwhile, pat scallops dry and salt them generously. Thoroughly heat an ovenproof nonstick skillet over medium-high heat, then sear the scallops. When the scallops appear bronzed at their base—after 2 or 3 minutes—add the butter and oil, turn the scallops, and transfer the skillet to the oven. Cook for 6 or 7 minutes or until medium-rare and well bronzed on both sides.

The potatoes will by now have absorbed much of the dressing; add more to taste and toss the salad again. Divide it among four plates or transfer to a single large platter, top with the scallops, and sprinkle with the remaining parsley.

Variations: This salad also works very well as a backdrop for butter-poached lobster (page 131) as well as fillets of red mullet, seared in a dry, salted pan skin side down, finished quickly in the oven, and served skin side up.

Suggested wine: Pouilly-Fuissé

Warm Beet Salad with Chèvre-Filled Phyllo Purse

The aesthetic appeal of this salad relies heavily upon a range of colours in the beets, so aim to combine on the plate as many varieties as possible (candy cane, golden, red cylinder, white, and so on). As for the flavours in play, every beet loves the company of goat cheese. We enhance that classic combination by wrapping the lightened chèvre in the flaky crunch of a phyllo pastry purse. SERVES 6

9 oz (250 g) fresh goat cheese
1 tsp (5 mL) minced sage
1 tbsp (15 mL) minced parsley
Pinch of minced rosemary
Salt and pepper
1 package (16 oz/454 g) phyllo pastry

3 tbsp (45 mL) butter, melted
20 to 24 young beets, about 2 lb (1 kg) total, baked and peeled (page 189)
½ cup (125 mL) maple-walnut vinaigrette (page 250)
Approximately 18 pieces oven-dried tomato (page 237)
1 handful each frisée and baby red leaf lettuce

Preheat oven to 350°F (180°F).

In a bowl mash the goat cheese with the sage, 1 tsp (5 mL) of the parsley, and the rosemary, and season lightly. Working quickly, cut the phyllo into 6 9-by-12-inch (22.5 by 30 cm) sheets and stack them under a damp kitchen towel. Remove one sheet and brush it with melted butter, top with a second sheet, brush again with butter, and then do the same with a third sheet. Cut the three-ply sheet lengthwise into strips about 3 inches (8 cm) wide. Return two three-ply strips to rest under the damp towel. Arrange one three-ply strip so that it faces away from you. Place a heaping tablespoonful of seasoned goat cheese towards the left hand side of the strip, about ½ inch (1 cm) in from the edges. Fold the right corner up at a 45-degree angle to cover the cheese. Then flip the cheese envelope upward so that the bottom of the strip is straight again. Continue folding until the cheese is completely sealed in a triangular package. Place the package flap side down on a baking sheet lined with parchment paper. Repeat to make five more packages. Brush the cheese purses with melted butter, sprinkle with the remaining parsley, and bake until golden—10 to 15 minutes.

Meanwhile, cut the beets into segments, then toss them with half the vinaigrette and arrange on a large platter. Scatter tomatoes and lettuce over the beets and then finish with the cheese purses. Serve with the extra dressing on the side.

Substitutions: Lemon-garlic or even sherry-shallot vinaigrette (page 250) are perfect substitutions for the maple-walnut vinaigrette.

Suggested wine: Sancerre

Variegated Heirloom Tomatoes with Olive Oil, Balsamic Vinegar, Basil, and Sea Salt

Cheap airfreight and hydroponics have together conspired to make us accustomed to eating whatever we please all year round. But there is greater pleasure to be derived from waiting for things to come into their proper season, and eating them only then, at their best. For me the list of things to look forward to is always topped by the tomato. At One, we celebrate its arrival with a salad built on an exuberance of colours, types, and sizes, cut into all sorts of different shapes, and simply dressed. **SERVES 4**

About 3 lb (1.5 kg) ripe heirloom tomatoes, all different varieties
2 tbsp (30 mL) fine olive oil
2 tsp (10 mL) fine aged balsamic (or balsamic reduction, page 232)
2 tsp (10 mL) best-quality mild sea salt (such as Maldon, sel gris de Guérande, or fleur de sel)
20 leaves basil, torn

Core the tomatoes and cut them into different shapes and sizes, slicing some, quartering others, and so on. Arrange them on a plate in a manner that best displays their broad array of colours. Drizzle with oil and balsamic, sprinkle with salt, and then scatter the basil over top.

Suggested wine: Sauvignon Blanc or Soave

Lentil Salad with Lardons, Blue Cheese, Cranberries, and Sherry-Shallot Vinaigrette

Toothsome lentils combine with the strong, creamy bite of blue cheese and the sweet counterpoint of dried cranberries in a salad that is filling, satisfying, and encouragingly healthful. It has been a bestseller at McEwan Fine Foods since very early days but is unlikely to remain so now that it has been revealed that it is so quick and easy to compose at home. **SERVES 6**

2 cups (500 mL) Puy lentils, picked over
1 cup (250 mL) diced top-quality bacon
1½ cups (375 mL) roughly chopped dried cranberries
3 oz (90 g) quality blue cheese (such as Saint Agur or Roquefort), crumbled
¼ cup (50 mL) chopped parsley
½ cup (125 mL) sherry-shallot vinaigrette (page 250)
Salt and pepper
6 leaves of Bibb lettuce

Simmer the lentils in salted water until just tender—15 to 20 minutes. Rinse, drain, and set aside in the refrigerator overnight.*

Slowly render the bacon until just crisp at the edges, then transfer to paper towels and let it cool slightly. Combine the lentils and bacon in a large bowl. Follow with the cranberries, blue cheese, parsley, vinaigrette, salt, and pepper. Combine well. Taste and correct seasonings. Serve on a bed of lettuce.

*If the lentils are not properly chilled before mixing the salad, their heat will liquefy the blue cheese and make a mess of things.

Suggested wine: Pinot Noir

Lobster Salad with Purslane, Japanese Pear, Grapefruit, and Cucumber with Crème Fraîche Dressing

Here sweet lobster meat finds pleasant contrast in the mildly salty bite of the purslane and the assertive crunch of Japanese pear. This is a very refreshing salad, with lots of citrus notes and bright fresh herbs, all bound together by a creamy crème fraîche vinaigrette. SERVES 2

1 large lobster, about 2½ lb (1.25 kg), fully cooked
(page 237), shelled, and chilled
1 tbsp (15 mL) yuzu dressing (page 251)
½ English cucumber, peeled, seeded, and cut into
¼-in (5 mm) dice
1 Japanese pear, cored and cut into ¼-in (5 mm) dice
½ tsp (2 mL) toasted sesame seeds
¼ tsp (1 mL) olive oil

2 small handfuls of purslane
8 grapefruit segments, membrane removed
1 tbsp (15 mL) crème fraîche dressing (page 251),
infused with a pinch of cayenne pepper
4 large leaves Belgian endive, top 3 in (8 cm) only
Leaves from 2 sprigs cilantro
Leaves from 1 sprig mint, torn
Leaves from 1 sprig basil, torn

Slice the lobster tail into discs about ½ inch (1 cm) thick, and toss in a bowl with the knuckle meat, whole claws, and half the yuzu dressing. Reserve.

In a separate bowl combine the cucumber, pear, sesame seeds, and olive oil, and toss. Place a 3-inch (8 cm) diameter mould at the centre of two chilled plates and divide the cucumber-pear salad between them. Remove the mould and top each tower with a cluster of purslane. Surround each with lobster tail discs and pieces of knuckle, and then rest a claw against the purslane, pincer end up. Distribute the grapefruit slices between the lobster pieces. Do the same with small dabs of the piquant crème fraîche dressing. Slice the endive leaves lengthwise into 3 or 4 strips each and scatter them over the plates. Drizzle the remaining yuzu dressing over the salads. Scatter them with the fresh herbs and serve.

Suggested wine: rich Chardonnay or exotic Viognier

Lobster Salad with Bacon and Blue Cheese

This salad plays with the notes drummed up by that classic American salad, the Cobb. We maintain the chorus (lettuce, tomato, avocado, bacon, blue cheese), but the confident assumption that there is almost nobody out there who does not believe that lobster is better than chicken gives it a new voice. SERVES 4

1 slab (5 oz/150 g) top-quality bacon, cut into ¼-in (5 mm) lardons
2 tbsp (30 mL) vegetable or olive oil
3 tbsp (45 mL) garlic butter*
4 thin slices of baguette, cut diagonally
1 head Bibb lettuce (preferably hydroponic)
12 sweet cherry tomatoes, halved
¼ red onion, sliced
3 radishes, thinly sliced
1 cup (250 mL) crème fraîche dressing (page 251)
1 ripe avocado, cubed
2 hard-boiled eggs, quartered
5 oz (150 g) Saint Agur or other top-quality blue cheese, crumbled
1 live lobster, about 1¼ lb (625 g), cooked and shelled (page 237),
    chilled, and cut into bite-size pieces
¼ bunch chives, cut into 2-in (5 cm) lengths

Slowly cook the bacon in the oil, without allowing it to get excessively crisp. Set aside to drain on paper towels. Spread garlic butter on the baguette slices and in a separate pan, fry them gently until golden. Set aside on paper towels. Put 12 to 16 whole leaves of lettuce, the tomatoes, onion, and radishes in a large bowl and toss with half the crème fraîche dressing. Place the largest four leaves of lettuce concave side up at the centre of four chilled plates. Follow with a judicious scattering of the dressed tomato, onion, and radish, along with avocado, egg segments, lardons, blue cheese, and lobster. Repeat the layers with lettuce leaves of diminishing size until each salad is three or four layers tall. Finish with an extra drizzle of dressing, the croutons, and the chives.

*If you don't have garlic butter handy, simply fry the croutons in ordinary butter with 3 or 4 smashed cloves of garlic sharing the pan.

Suggested wine: crisp Chardonnay

Octopus and Calamari Salad with Chili-Citrus Dressing

Given the frequency of our encounters with bland and rubbery octopus, you might well think that it is particularly complicated to cook—but not so. This method, wherein the slow simmer is followed by a light char on the grill, yields an unfailingly supple and flavoursome result. When combined with calamari and young greens and enlivened with a piquant dressing, it translates into Bymark's most popular salad. SERVES 4

2 whole octopi, about 4 lb (2 kg) total, cleaned
2 quarts (2 L) court bouillon (page 246)
4 squid, about 7 oz (200 g) total, cleaned
½ cup (125 mL) chili-citrus dressing (page 250)
4 serving portions of young greens (some combination of mustard, Osaka mustard, frisée, onion cress, and lolla rossa)

¼ celery root, peeled and julienned
12 celery leaves
8 chives, quartered
1½ tbsp (23 mL) finely diced red and yellow bell pepper
Pinch of salt
4 tsp (20 mL) lemon-garlic vinaigrette (page 250)

Lay octopi flat on a cutting board, with the head at centre and the arms stretched outwards. With a mallet or hammer, lightly pound the legs—no harder than you would knock on a door—until they feel tender. Add octopi to a pot of court bouillon and bring to a slow simmer. After 45 minutes test for tenderness by inserting a knife where the arms join the head. It should penetrate easily—if not, continue cooking until it does, testing every 10 minutes or so. When done, remove octopi and let cool. Cut arms from head and discard head. Then scrape away the rough skin from the back of the arms as well as some of the peripheral suction cups. If not using octopi immediately, refrigerate.

Preheat grill to high.

Ensure the squid are properly cleaned by trimming the legs and bodies and checking the cavity for cartilage. Oil the grill rack, and cook the squid for about a minute on one side, then flip them and add the octopus, cooking it for about 30 seconds per side. Transfer the octopus and squid heads to a bowl. Transfer the squid bodies to a cutting board, slice them into rings about ½ inch (1 cm) thick, and add to the bowl. Add about two-thirds of the chili-citrus dressing and toss well.

Divide the greens among four plates, placing them to one side. Top each portion with 6 batonets of celery root, 3 celery leaves, and 8 chive sticks. Arrange seafood alongside. Sprinkle the bell peppers over the seafood, add a final squirt of chili-citrus dressing and a pinch of salt, and lastly, adorn the greens with lemon-garlic dressing.

Suggested wine: Spätlese or off-dry Riesling

First Courses

At a restaurant the first course is in many ways the most important, for it sets the tone for the meal. Yet even when it is a success, and completely fulfilling, its job is still to leave the diner wanting more. That takes balance. Many chefs get carried away out of the starting gate, firing off their best shots too soon and setting up their main course to be a letdown.

Your approach to dinner at home is, I hope, a little more relaxed. But all the same, the first course gets the most attention, if only because you serve it when everyone is hungriest. Here we have brought together some of the very finest first courses ever to appear on the menus at North 44, Bymark, and One, simplified slightly to make them more manageable and convenient for the home cook. Some are nonetheless better suited to the weekend project than for tackling after work—but each is a certified great start to a great meal.

Tuna Tataki with Yuzu

Right down to the yuzu juice, this dish draws its inspiration rather obviously from the incomparable Nobuyuki Matsuhisa—more commonly known as Nobu. Japanese cuisine is another world, but even if your familiarity with its technique is slight, there is no reason to shy away from preparing this simple and exceptional dish, as long as you have a good source for top-quality tuna. SERVES 2

1 piece best-quality tuna loin, about 3 oz (90 g)
Salt
1 tbsp (15 mL) sesame crust (page 244)
2 tsp (10 mL) butter
1 tbsp (15 mL) yuzu dressing (page 251)
1 tsp (5 mL) fragrant soy (page 234)
6 paper-thin slices of jalapeño, seeded
6 cilantro leaves

Salt the tuna generously and then allow it to rest for 10 minutes. Pat excess water from the tuna by dabbing it with a paper towel. Spread the sesame crust on a work surface and roll the tuna through it to coat. Thoroughly heat a small nonstick skillet on high heat, lubricate it with the butter, then sear the tuna for no more than 15 seconds on any given side. Transfer the tuna to the refrigerator until well chilled.

Slice the tuna into 6 slices—about ¼ inch (5 mm)—and arrange them side by side on a cold plate. Drizzle with yuzu dressing and soy, then place one slice of jalapeño and one leaf of cilantro on top of each piece of fish. Serve.

Substitutions: Red tuna looks prettiest mingling with the other colours at play in this dish, but what with yellowfin and bluefin stocks being in such desperate shape, the best choice is albacore tuna sourced from the coast of B.C., for this flavourful white tuna is in enviably healthy supply.

Suggested wine: tropical Gavi or New Zealand Sauvignon Blanc

Woodland Mushroom Tart with Frisée

This small, light mushroom quiche makes a lovely first course for a summer luncheon, especially when topped with a small salad of frisée with walnuts. But remember that in the end it is essentially a vehicle for the mushrooms within; pedestrian cultivated mushrooms make a dull tart that is not worth the trouble. SERVES 6

1 batch pâte brisée (page 239)
3 eggs
1½ cups (375 mL) 35% cream
2 cups (500 mL) mixed woodland mushrooms,
    sautéed (page 179)
½ cup (125 mL) crumbled goat cheese
1 tbsp (15 mL) mixed minced parsley and thyme

Salt and pepper
1 small bunch frisée, torn
6 basil leaves, torn
Leaves from 2 sprigs Italian parsley
6 walnuts
2 tsp (10 mL) maple-walnut vinaigrette
    (page 250)

Preheat oven to 375°F (190°C).

On a floured work surface, roll out pâte brisée to a thickness of about ⅛ inch (3 mm). Cut portions to line six small tart pans about 3 inches (8 cm) in diameter. Trim the edges, line the tart shells with foil, fill them with pebbles or dried beans, and transfer to a baking sheet. Bake until golden at the edges—about 15 minutes. Remove the foil and weights. Lightly beat 1 egg and brush the insides of the tart shells. Return them to the oven until completely golden—another 5 to 8 minutes. Set aside to cool. Lower oven to 325°F (160°C).

Combine the remaining 2 eggs and cream in the bowl of a stand mixer and whisk at medium-low speed until the mixture begins to thicken—3 to 5 minutes. Fill the cooled tart crusts about half—or at most, two-thirds—of the way to their tops with the cooked mushrooms. Add to each a generous tablespoonful of goat cheese, a pinch of mixed herbs, and a dash of seasoning. Next, pour in the egg mixture to cover. Bake until lightly bronzed on top and well set in the centre—35 to 40 minutes. Let tarts rest for 10 minutes.

Meanwhile, combine the frisée, basil, parsley, and walnuts in a bowl. Immediately before serving, toss with the vinaigrette. Serve tarts with a light cluster of the salad mounded on top.

Variation: You can of course simplify matters by baking a single large tart and portioning it by slice. Alternatively, you can turn the recipe into an elegant side dish for any main course that goes well with mushrooms or cheese. Simply reduce the quantities and fill miniature tart shells about 1½ inches (4 cm) wide. The cooking time will be about 5 minutes shorter.

Substitutions: If time or will is lacking for making pâte brisée, a quality store-bought frozen brand will work fine as a substitute. So too will good-quality store-bought tart shells. Lastly, while the walnut-dressed frisée is a lovely complement, any delicate salad and dressing will do.

Suggested wine: Pinot Noir or Chardonnay

Terrine of Foie Gras

Foie gras from Quebec farms like Palmex, Élevages Périgord, and Canard Goulu is collectively one of the great Canadian food products and a source of considerable culinary prestige abroad (except maybe for in Chicago). While all foie gras terrines are by nature pleasing, the particular manner of assembling this one—in layers—produces a pâté of particularly pleasing aesthetic as well as exceptional smoothness. Single-handedly, it improves Christmas.
MAKES ABOUT 2½ LB (1.25 KG) TERRINE, ENOUGH FOR 20 TO 30 SERVINGS

2 whole lobes of fresh Grade A foie gras,
    about 1½ lb (750 g) each
2 cups (500 mL) dry sherry
⅓ cup (75 mL) salt
3 tbsp (45 mL) granulated sugar
2 tsp (10 mL) finely ground white pepper
2 tsp (5 mL) saltpetre
2 quarts (2 L) whole milk
Black truffles (optional)

RECOMMENDED ACCOMPANIMENTS: Pickled pears (page 240), pear-vanilla chutney (page 240), port jelly (page 240), and fresh brioche

Rinse the lobes of foie gras well under the coldest possible running water, pat dry with paper towels, and transfer to a tall-sided container large enough to accommodate them in a single layer. Simmer the sherry briefly to evaporate its alcohol, then set aside to cool in the refrigerator. Mix together the salt, sugar, white pepper, and saltpetre. Combine ¼ cup (50 mL) of the seasoning mixture with the milk and the chilled sherry, pour it over the foie gras, cover, and marinate in the refrigerator for 24 hours.

Remove the foie gras from their marinade and once again rinse them under cold water and pat dry. Cover with plastic wrap and let rest at room temperature for 30 to 45 minutes—until they lose their stiffness and become pliable to the touch. Working with one liver at a time, transfer it flat side up to a work surface to be deveined. Begin by gently breaking the liver into two constituent lobes, and then follow the vein that held them together, pulling it away from the tissue with tweezers or prying it out with a sharp skewer as you follow it to its root-like ends, working forcefully enough to tear the tissue but not so much as to break and lose the vein.

Line a baking sheet with plastic wrap and sprinkle it with some of the seasoning mixture. Transfer the livers to the baking sheet side by side, sprinkle lightly with the seasoning mixture, and cover with plastic wrap. You should have one joined layer of foie gras about ¾ inch (2 cm) thick. If there are breaks or tears, press around them gently to work the tissue back together. If there are lumps, flatten them. Then place another baking sheet on top, weight it, and transfer to the refrigerator for another 24 hours.

Preheat oven to 325°F (160°C).

continued

Measure the bottom of your terrine mould. Cut a rectangle of the same size from the flattened foie gras. Season the bottom of the mould with a sprinkling of the seasoning mixture and place the rectangle of foie gras on top. Fill in any holes with trimmings, and then use the back of a warm spoon to press the layer of liver as flat as possible, ridding it of air holes and ensuring that it meets the sides of the mould. Sprinkle with seasoning mix, and if desired, top with a layer of truffle shavings. Then repeat, applying layer after seasoned layer until the foie gras is all gone and the mould is nearly full. Cover with foil and the lid.

Prepare a bain-marie with warm water and heat it in the oven for 15 minutes. Transfer the terrine to the bain-marie and bake for 20 to 25 minutes—or until the internal temperature at the centre registers 130°F (55°C). Transfer the terrine to an ice bath to cool for 10 to 15 minutes. Then uncover it, place a weight on top of the foil, place it on a baking sheet to catch drips, and chill for at least 24 hours.

To remove the terrine from the mould, run a knife around the edge, warm the mould briefly in hot water, and invert it very carefully. Trim the terrine of any excess fat, wrap it in plastic wrap, and chill it again before slicing it with a warm knife.

Substitutions: White port can be substituted for the sherry. If saltpetre is unavailable, use extra salt in its place.

Suggested wine: Riesling, Champagne, or Sauternes

Truffle Pizza

This is *pizza bianco* royalty. The inspiration came from a truffle pizza by Jean-Georges Vongerichten, but at North 44 we came up with a different execution, opting for a thinner crust and a more measured application of truffle. You can make individual pizzas for a first course or just make one or two to divide as a luxurious snack to enjoy with the aperitifs.
MAKES ENOUGH FOR 6

1 package (8 g) active dry yeast (or 25 g fresh yeast)
2 eggs
3½ cups (875 mL) flour, sifted
1½ tbsp (23 mL) salt
¼ cup (50 mL) olive oil
½ cup (125 mL) truffle paste
5 oz (150 g) fontina cheese, shredded
1 small truffle, about 1½ oz (40 g)
1 small bunch frisée, separated
Truffle oil (optional)

Proof the yeast according to the manufacturer's instructions. Place the eggs in their shells in a bowl of warm water for 5 minutes. Transfer activated yeast to the bowl of a stand mixer with 2½ cups (625 mL) of the flour, the eggs, salt, 2 tbsp (30 mL) of the olive oil, and ¾ cup (175 mL) warm water. Blend with a dough hook on low speed. Once it is well mixed and has balled together, feel the dough. If it is sticky, add more flour and work it again. You want the dough to be tacky to the touch but not sticky. Let the dough rest in a covered bowl on the countertop for 2 hours.

Preheat grill to high and oven to 450°F (230°C).

Mix truffle paste with the remaining olive oil. Roll out dough on a floured surface, stretching it out into oblongs of desired size. For each pizza, oil the grill rack, and place the dough directly on top of the freshly lubricated surface. As soon as the first side crisps, flip it over and cook the second. Then remove the pizza crust to a work surface and smear or brush it with the diluted truffle paste. Sprinkle it generously with shredded cheese and transfer to the oven just long enough for the cheese to melt—1 to 2 minutes. While the cheese is still piping hot, shave the truffle over the pizza to taste. Follow with a sprinkling of frisée sprigs and, if desired, a scattering of truffle oil. Enjoy at once.

Suggested wine: Pinot Noir or Nebbiolo

Gravlax with Sweet Potato Pancakes and Mustard-Spiked Crème Fraîche

This classic Scandinavian dish relies on a good cure, especially nowadays when the salmon we use is almost always farmed and considerably fattier than the better exercised wild fish that came before. This recipe from Bymark delivers a reliably superior result, and when paired with these sweet, richly flavoured pancakes never fails to please. SERVES 12

GRAVLAX
2 oz (60 mL) brandy
1 oz (30 mL) liquid honey
2 cups (500 mL) kosher salt
1 cup (250 mL) granulated sugar
¾ cup (175 mL) brown sugar
1 top-quality Atlantic salmon fillet, 3½ lb (1.6 kg),
  skin on, pin bones removed
1 tsp (5 mL) pepper
Zest of ½ orange
Zest of ½ lemon
1½ cups (375 mL) chopped dill

PANCAKES
1 small Yukon Gold potato
½ medium sweet potato
2 cups (500 mL) flour
2½ tbsp (40 mL) brown sugar

1 egg
2 cups (500 mL) milk
½ cup (125 mL) 18% cream
¼ cup (50 mL) sour cream
1 tbsp (15 mL) butter, melted
1 tbsp (15 mL) molasses
2 tsp (5 mL) kosher salt
½ tsp (2 mL) white pepper
1 tsp (5 mL) baking powder
2 tbsp (30 mL) butter

GARNISH
1 lemon
¼ cup (50 mL) Dijon mustard
1 cup (250 mL) crème fraîche (page 231)
2 tbsp (30 mL) finely minced red onion
Dill sprigs

GRAVLAX: In a small saucepan, heat the brandy, flame it, stir in the honey, and set aside to cool. Meanwhile, combine the salt and two sugars in a large bowl and mix well, breaking up all the clumps. Sprinkle half the mixture over an area slightly larger than the salmon fillet in a container with sides at least 2 inches (5 cm) high. Place the salmon on top, skin side down, gently stretching it out to maximize its exposure. Sprinkle the pepper over the fish, followed by the orange and lemon zests. Follow with the dill and the remainder of the salt-sugar mixture. Drizzle with the honeyed brandy. Seal the container with plastic wrap, place a weight on top to press the fish, and refrigerate for 48 hours.

PANCAKES: Preheat oven to 375°F (190°C). Roast the Yukon and sweet potatoes until they are soft inside, about 45 minutes. Peel, pass through a fine-mesh sieve, and set aside. Combine the flour and sugar in a bowl. In a separate large bowl, lightly beat the egg, then add the milk, cream, sour cream, butter, and molasses. Stir the dry ingredients into the wet, then fold in the riced potatoes, salt, and pepper until smooth and well combined. Let the batter rest (ideally overnight).

Shortly before serving, adjust the batter seasonings, then whisk in the baking powder. Heat a large nonstick pan over medium-low heat. Add a little of the butter, spread it thinly around the pan with a brush or paper towel, and then pour in pancake batter to make 2-inch (5 cm) rounds. Cook like ordinary pancakes, adding more butter as necessary, and set aside. Continue until you have about 50 pancakes.

Rinse the salmon under cold running water, working it gently with your fingers to dislodge crystallized salt and sugar but not all the dill and zest. Pat dry. If the fillet extends to the tail, remove the bottom 3 inches (8 cm). Cut thin slices of salmon at a 45-degree angle towards the tail, turning your knife upwards before it gets too close to the skin. Cut extremely thin slices of lemon and cut into individual segments. Use a thin, sharp knife to fillet the segments of citrus from their surrounding membrane and pith. Stir the mustard into the crème fraîche and add a few drops of lemon juice to taste.

To serve as a plated appetizer, place a stack of 3 or 4 pancakes to one side of the plate, arrange ruffled slices of salmon alongside, scatter with onion, lemon segments, and dill sprigs, and finish with a ramekin of crème fraîche. Alternatively, to serve as a passed hors d'oeuvre, assemble individual pancakes, topping each rosette of salmon with a dollop of crème fraîche, onion, lemon, and dill.

Suggested wine: Champagne or Chardonnay

Seared Foie Gras with Toasted Brioche, Macerated Cherries, Praline, and Dark Chocolate

Seared foie gras is by nature an indulgent dish, and if you are going there you might as well go all the way. At North 44 we do that by embellishing the classic combination of foie gras, brioche, and braised fruit with crunchily satisfying candied praline and the bitter counterpoint of dark chocolate. And then for good measure we add a little foie gras foam—which is optional here. SERVES 6

1 cup (250 mL) simple syrup (page 244)
1 lb (450 g) sweet cherries, halved and pitted
1 cup (250 ml) veal jus (page 247)
6 brioche rounds, ¼ in (5 mm) thick and 2½ in (6 cm) in diameter
6 thick slices top-quality foie gras, about 3 oz (90 g) each

Salt
2 tbsp (30 mL) chopped candied pistachio praline (page 229)
18 crispy sage leaves (page 180)
1 tbsp (15 mL) whipped butter (page 251)
1 cup (250 mL) foie gras foam (optional; page 232)
3 tsp (15 mL) grated dark chocolate

Reduce the simple syrup by half, then add the cherries and simmer for 3 minutes. Remove half the cherry-infused simple syrup to a small saucepan and reduce by half. Set aside the remaining cherries in their braising liquid.

Warm the veal jus. Toast the brioche slices, butter them, and keep warm.

Lightly score the foie gras on one side. Thoroughly heat a heavy-bottomed skillet over medium-high heat. Generously salt the scored side of the foie gras and place in the hot skillet scored side down. Salt the second side while the liver sears—for 60 to 90 seconds. Drain fat from the pan and flip the foie gras. Sear the second side for 60 seconds.

Meanwhile, begin plating. Spoon a cluster of warm cherries along with a little of their braising liquid at the centre of six warm plates. Then perch a piece of toasted brioche over the cherries and top that with the seared foie gras. Sprinkle with candied praline and crispy sage leaves. Add the whipped butter to the veal jus, froth with a hand wand, and pour around the foie gras. Then, if you so choose, top with a generous dollop of foie gras foam. Finish with a scattering of chocolate shavings and a drizzle of cherry syrup.

*The ideal thickness of a slice of foie gras for searing is 1 inch (2.5 cm). At that size you should remove it from the refrigerator and allow it to approach room temperature before dropping it into a hot skillet. But if you purchased the foie gras pre-sliced and it was cut substantially thinner, cook it cold or else the centre will overcook before the outside is properly browned.

Substitutions: Candied walnuts or hazelnuts—prepared in an identical manner—can be used in place of the pistachios. For the cherries, you may substitute another seasonal fruit similarly prepared—like Riesling-braised apples (page 227), peaches, or pears.

Suggested wine: Sauternes or Champagne

Bison Tartare

Like any lean and tender meat, bison tenderloin is eminently suitable for turning into tartare. Its crimson hue is an aesthetic bonus. Do not let health concerns prevent you from making tartare at home, but do remember two simple rules: Always keep the meat well chilled until the very last minute before serving—and only then, chop it yourself, by hand. SERVES 4

½ cup (125 mL) canola or vegetable oil
1 tbsp (15 mL) capers, rinsed, dried on paper towels
1 lb (450 g) bison tenderloin
1 whole scallion, minced
2½ tbsp (40 mL) minced shallot
1 tbsp (15 mL) minced red radish
1 tbsp (15 mL) chopped pickled beet
1 tbsp (15 mL) grainy mustard
1 tbsp (15 mL) olive oil

1 egg yolk
1 tsp (5 mL) Worcestershire sauce
1 tsp (5 mL) lemon juice
Salt and pepper
1 tsp (5 mL) minced chives
1 tsp (5 mL) minced parsley

GARNISH
4 raw quail egg yolks in the half-shell

SUGGESTED ACCOMPANIMENTS: Young greens or frisée, toasted thin diagonal slices of baguette; or serve as a main course for two with Perfect French fries (page 194)

Heat the canola oil in small skillet until it nearly arrives at its smoking point. Add the capers and fry until they burst, then quickly transfer them with a slotted spoon to paper towels to drain. Working as quickly as possible, chop the bison thoroughly, and then transfer it to a bowl. Add the scallion, shallot, radish, beet, mustard, olive oil, egg yolk, Worcestershire sauce, and lemon juice. Season and mix well. Taste and adjust seasonings. Divide into mini burger–like portions, sprinkle with crispy capers, chives, and parsley, top with the quail eggs, and serve with selected accompaniments.

Variations: The same preparation applies equally well to other lean, quality cuts of game meat, from bear to moose and venison, and even horse. For steak tartare, use beef tenderloin; instead of pickled beet and radish, use 4 minced gherkins and a good splash of Tabasco sauce.

Suggested wine: soft, young red or a rich, full-bodied white

Warm Autumn Salad with Wild Mushrooms, Truffles, Quail Eggs, and Garlic Toast

This lovely warm salad clusters all of the pungent, earthy flavours of autumn on one elegant plate. Replicating this perfect dish in the home kitchen is not the least bit difficult. By all means, do spring for the truffle—it makes the dish. SERVES 2

4 slices ciabatta (or baguette cut diagonally), ¼ in (5 mm) thick
2 cups (500 mL) finest wild mushrooms, cleaned and trimmed
1 tbsp (15 mL) olive oil
Salt and pepper
1 tbsp (15 mL) Italian soffritto (page 244)
¼ cup (50 mL) white chicken stock (page 246)
½ tbsp (7 mL) minced chives
1 tbsp (15 mL) whipped butter (page 251)
1 tbsp (15 mL) truffle paste
2 quail eggs, soft-poached
Shavings of Manchego
Truffle shavings (optional)
2 small bunches young greens
A few drops of olive oil and lemon juice

Butter and pan-crisp the ciabatta slices; set aside, keeping warm.

Meanwhile, sauté the mushrooms in oil over medium-high heat for 2 to 3 minutes. Season lightly, and then add the soffritto. Toss, and sauté a minute longer. When the mushrooms have softened, deglaze with half the chicken stock. Stir in the chives. Remove the pan from the heat, add the butter, and stir gently to encourage its absorption. If the mixture appears dry, add a touch more chicken stock and stir to incorporate. Add the truffle paste and stir until creamy.

Place one warm, crisp slice of toast near the centre of each plate. Heap the mushrooms on the toast, then top with a second slice of toast. Top with a quail egg, then Manchego shavings, and finally—if available—truffle shavings. Lightly dress young greens in oil and lemon juice and place a cluster alongside the warm salad.

Variation: Two portions—or more—can be more casually plated family-style on one large serving dish, in which case a single conventional poached egg can easily stand in for the smaller ones sourced from the quail.

Suggested wine: earthy Chardonnay, Pinot Noir

Game Terrine with Rabbit and Squab

The art of charcuterie takes many years to master. This terrine, however, does not require any great skill—only a little finesse, a fair bit of time, and the right kitchen equipment. The results are sublime. MAKES ABOUT 3 LB (1.5 KG) TERRINE, ENOUGH FOR ABOUT 24 PLATED SERVINGS

1 rabbit, about 3½ lb (1.6 kg)
4 shallots—1 sliced, 3 minced
1 cup (250 mL) white wine
1 medium carrot, sliced
1 celery stalk, sliced
1 small leek, sliced
8 black peppercorns
4 bay leaves
2 squab, about 1¼ lb (625 g) each, boned
2 tbsp (30 mL) olive oil
Salt and white pepper
¼ cup (50 mL) vegetable oil
1 rabbit liver (or 3 oz/90 g chicken livers)
1 tbsp (15 mL) garlic, minced
3 tbsp (45 mL) ground dried juniper berries
2 tbsp (30 mL) ground toasted coriander seeds
2 tbsp (30 mL) ground toasted yellow mustard seeds
5 whole cloves, toasted and ground
1 tbsp (15 mL) black peppercorns, ground
2½ oz (70 g) pork back fat, finely diced
2½ oz (70 g) fresh foie gras, cut in large dice
1 tbsp (15 mL) saltpetre
4 sprigs thyme
12 sheets (4 by 6 in/10 by 15 cm) very thinly sliced pork back fat

SUGGESTED ACCOMPANIMENTS: Good bread, mustard, gherkins

Bone (or ask your butcher to bone) the rabbit, beginning by removing the legs, and then very carefully filleting the two loins intact from the back (keeping them whole is essential to the structure of the terrine). Reserve the bones. Toss the loins with the sliced shallot and wine, then marinate in the refrigerator for at least 3 hours. Meanwhile, bring the rabbit bones to a boil with the carrot, celery, leek, peppercorns, and 1 bay leaf, then skim, lower the heat, and simmer, uncovered, until ½ cup (125 mL) of liquid remains. Strain into a container, discarding the solids, and refrigerate the stock until it coagulates.

continued

Spread the squab and remaining rabbit on a work surface, sprinkle with the olive oil and season generously. Heat a large nonstick skillet on high. Add the vegetable oil, and then barely sear the rabbit, squab, and rabbit liver on all sides. Remove meat to a baking sheet and refrigerate until cool. Meanwhile, sweat the minced shallot and garlic in a little olive oil until translucent, and then refrigerate until cool. Combine the juniper, coriander, mustard, cloves, and peppercorns.

Pass the rabbit, squab, and liver through a meat grinder fitted with a coarse blade—about ¼ inch (5 mm)—into a large bowl. Add the diced pork fat and foie gras. Chop the rabbit stock roughly and add that too. Follow with half the ground seasoning mixture and all the saltpetre. Mix well with a rubber spatula. Remove a small meatball-sized sample of the meat, sear it, and taste. It should taste very generously seasoned, for the effect will be dulled when the terrine is served chilled. If not, add more of the seasoning. Set mixture aside in the refrigerator.

Preheat oven to 300°F (150°C).

Dress the bottom of a lidded 5-cup (1.25 L) terrine mould with the thyme sprigs and remaining 3 bay leaves. Then line the mould with the sheets of back fat, positioning them lengthwise perpendicular to the terrine, overlapping in its base and overhanging its sides. Half fill the mould with the meat mixture, pressing down with the back of a spoon to expel any air pockets. Place the marinated rabbit loins on top, with their narrow ends overlapping at the centre so that their meat is an even width along the entire length of the terrine. Press them down lightly into the mixture. Fill the terrine with the remaining meat mixture, pressing down once again to eliminate any air pockets. Now flip the fat over the top of the terrine so that they completely cover the meat. Trim any excessive overlap with sharp scissors.

Cover the terrine with foil and its lid and then place it in a bain-marie. Bake for 60 to 75 minutes, checking the internal temperature after 1 hour. When the temperature at the centre of the terrine reads 130°F (55°C), transfer it to an ice bath to arrest the cooking. Once chilled, transfer it to the refrigerator for at least 24 hours.

Before serving, place the mould briefly in hot water to loosen the terrine, then uncover it and carefully invert it onto a platter.

Substitutions: If squab is unavailable, duck can be used in its place—but it must be the relatively lean meat of the magret. Ordinary salt can be used instead of saltpetre, but saltpetre is a superior preservative.

Suggested wine: Côtes du Rhône or Pinot Noir

Seared Sea Scallops with Crisp Pancetta and Beluga Lentils

Here we pair the scallop with pancetta and cook the two separately so that the flavours are combined but each element is cooked in its individually ideal manner. SERVES 4

3 tbsp (30 mL) olive oil
½ cup (125 mL) minced onion
1 tbsp (15 mL) minced garlic
1 cup (250 mL) beluga lentils, picked over
½ cup (125 mL) white wine
3 cups (750 mL) white chicken stock (page 246)
4 medium carrots, scrubbed
Salt and pepper
10 leaves Bibb lettuce, halved, ribs removed,
    cut into chiffonade
3 scallions, green part only, cut into chiffonade
2 tbsp (30 mL) whipped butter (page 251)
1 tbsp (15 mL) minced chives

SCALLOPS
8 dry-packed sea scallops
Salt
1½ tbsp (23 mL) butter
1 tsp (5 mL) olive oil

GARNISH
8 slices crisp pancetta (page 231), each broken into
    2 or 3 pieces
Sprigs of watercress or other decorative greens
¼ cup (50 mL) frothed butter sauce (optional; page 229)

Place a medium saucepan over medium-low heat, heat 2 tbsp (30 mL) of the olive oil, and then add the onions. Salt lightly and sweat for 5 to 7 minutes, until translucent. Stir in the garlic. A minute later add the lentils, stir well, and deglaze with the wine. Add 1 cup (250 mL) of the chicken stock and bring to a simmer. Stir regularly, adding more stock ½ cup (125 mL) at a time as the mixtures thickens, until the lentils are tender—45 to 60 minutes. Set aside.

Preheat oven to 400°F (200°C).

In an ovenproof skillet, sauté the carrots in the remaining 1 tbsp (15 mL) of oil for 1 to 2 minutes. Then salt generously, toss, and transfer the pan to the oven until the carrots are barely tender—6 or 7 minutes. Remove carrots from the pan to cool. Increase oven temperature to 450°F (230°C).

SCALLOPS: Pat scallops dry and salt them generously. Thoroughly heat an ovenproof nonstick skillet over medium-high heat, then sear the scallops. When they appear bronzed at the base—after 2 to 3 minutes—add the butter and oil, turn the scallops, and transfer the skillet to the oven. Cook for 6 or 7 minutes or until medium-rare and well bronzed on both sides.

Meanwhile, slice the carrots diagonally into discs roughly ⅛ inch (3 mm) thick. Fold the carrots into the tender-braised lentils along with the chiffonade of lettuce and scallion. Simmer until the greens are completely wilted. Adjust seasonings. Stir in butter and chives and divide among four plates. Top each serving with a pair of scallops. Garnish with a scattering of pancetta and watercress sprigs. If desired, douse each scallop in frothed butter sauce.

Suggested wine: New World Pinot Noir

Crispy-Fried Soft-Shell Crab with White Asparagus and Hollandaise

Nothing signals the long-awaited advent of spring quite like this exquisite crustacean mange-tout: the soft-shell crab. Butter is its best friend, so we deliver that with it in abundance. And then we add that other great bellwether of warm days to come—asparagus.

SERVES 6

2 cups (500 mL) flour
¼ cup (50 mL) salt
2 tsp (10 mL) Spanish sweet paprika
1 tsp (5 mL) cayenne pepper
6 live soft-shell crabs, cleaned and drained
2 cups (500 mL) clarified butter
3 ripe Roma tomatoes, cored, seeded, and diced
1 tbsp (15 mL) finely diced red onion
1 tbsp (15 mL) minced cilantro leaves

1 tbsp (15 mL) olive oil
2 tbsp (30 mL) red wine vinegar
Pinch each of salt and pepper
24 spears white asparagus, cooked (page 183)
1 cup (250 mL) hollandaise sauce (page 236)
12 pink grapefruit segments, membranes removed

GARNISH
Small sprigs of basil, parsley, or chervil

In a bowl combine the flour, salt, paprika, and cayenne. Transfer mixture to a baking sheet or large plate. Dredge the crabs in the seasoned flour, shake off excess, and set aside. Heat two large skillets over medium heat and divide the butter between them. When it is hot, add 3 crabs to each pan, starting them upside down. The butter should be hot enough to bubble but not to blacken the batter. When the crabs redden and crisp—after about 3 minutes—turn and repeat, then remove to drain on paper towels.

Combine the tomatoes, onion, and cilantro in a bowl. Add the oil, vinegar, salt, and pepper and toss.

Cut the claws from each crab at the base of the knuckle, then halve the torsos lengthwise. Arrange 4 asparagus spears in a row on each plate and stack crab on top, starting with the claws. Scatter with a little tomato salsa, spoon 2 tbsp (30 mL) hollandaise to one side, add 2 grapefruit segments, and garnish.

Variations: If you cannot find live soft-shell crab, you are well advised to forgo the frozen ones of inferior texture and instead use butter-poached lobster (page 131) or steamed prawns. To serve 6, use 3 lobster (about 1½ lb/750 g each), or 24 to 30 prawns.

Suggested wine: rich Vouvray or oaked Chardonnay

Whitefish Ceviche

This ceviche marinade strikes all the right bright notes for a refreshing snack on a sunny summer afternoon. It is highly versatile and so can be applied unaltered to any quality whitefish—or even salmon, char, scallops, or shrimp. SERVES 4

1 lb (450 g) skinless grouper fillet,
    cut into ¼-in (5 mm) dice
Juice of 3 limes
Juice of ½ orange
2 scallions, minced
½ cup (125 mL) minced onion
¼ cup (50 mL) minced cilantro
1 tbsp (15 mL) minced fresh ginger
1 tbsp (15 mL) soy sauce
3 Thai chilies, seeded and minced
½ tsp (2 mL) minced garlic
Salt

SUGGESTED ACCOMPANIMENTS: Bibb lettuce, flatbread, or tortilla chips

Combine the grouper, citrus juices, scallions, onion, cilantro, ginger, soy sauce, chilies, and garlic in a bowl. Stir, cover, and set aside for 5 minutes on the kitchen counter (or 10 to 15 in the refrigerator). Taste, correct seasonings, and serve.

Suggested wine: dry Riesling or mineral-rich Loire whites

Bacon and Eggs with Truffles

When at One in the Hazelton Hotel we put our minds to elevating the simple breakfast, our thoughts naturally enough turned to fluffier eggs, better (larger) bacon, and truffles. Consumed in bed, it makes a perfect start to a lazy morning. And what works for room service at the hotel is just as enjoyable at home. SERVES 2

4 oz (125 g) side bacon, cut into large lardons
1 tbsp (15 mL) olive oil
3 eggs, at room temperature
1 tsp (5 mL) crème fraîche (page 231)
1 tsp (5 mL) butter
1 tsp (5 mL) pork jus (optional; page 249)
¼ tsp (1 mL) minced chives
Salt and pepper
Truffle shavings to taste

Gently render the lardons in olive oil over low heat until lightly crisp, then set them aside to drain on paper towels. Whip the eggs vigorously for several minutes. Add the crème fraîche and whip them some more. Heat a skillet over low heat, add the butter, and when it has melted follow with the eggs. Cook to the desired doneness, stirring them constantly. Transfer to warm plates. Stud with the lardons, drizzle with pork jus if desired, sprinkle with chives, season—and finally, scatter with truffles.

Suggested wine: Champagne

Ceviche-Style Scallop Carpaccio

This extremely simple and quick recipe makes for a lovely light starter in warm weather. This subtle dish is all about the scallop, though; if you cannot procure plump, incontestably fresh dry-packed scallops, the recipe simply will not work. SERVES 6

½ English cucumber, peeled, seeded, and diced
1 tsp (5 mL) salt
1 tsp (5 mL) yuzu juice
9 dry-packed sea scallops, about 2½ oz (70 g) each
¼ tsp (1 mL) finely minced garlic
¼ tsp (1 mL) finely minced fresh ginger
Pinch of white pepper

1 jalapeño, very thinly sliced
1 red Thai chili, very thinly sliced
1 red radish, halved lengthwise and very thinly sliced
12 lemon segments, membranes removed
20 cilantro leaves
Small bunch small red shiso (optional)
Leaves from 1 bunch celery, torn

In a bowl, toss the cucumber with half the salt and half the yuzu juice, and set aside in the refrigerator. Slice the scallops into discs roughly ⅛ inch (3 mm) thick—about 6 per scallop. Toss with the remaining yuzu, garlic, ginger, and a pinch of salt and pepper. Refrigerate for 30 minutes.

Drain cucumber on paper towels and then scatter about 1 tbsp (15 mL) on each of six chilled plates. Top with a circle of scallop discs. Scatter each plate with a few slices of jalapeño, Thai chili, and radish, 2 lemon segments, and the cilantro, shiso if using, and celery leaves.

Substitutions: The juice of the yuzu enjoys a distinctive complementary relationship with raw fish—but lime juice or lemon juice will work as a stand-in if necessary.

Suggested wine: crisp Sauvignon Blanc

Lobster Poutine

A good forty years after the owner of a fast-food restaurant in Drummondville, Quebec, had the dubious culinary epiphany of combining French fries, cheese curds, and gravy, a handful of real Quebec chefs put their minds to turning *le snack national* into something you might eat with a silver-plated fork instead of a plastic one. So began the unlikely mingling of frites and foie gras. Our inspired cheese-free take instead stars lobster and béarnaise. SERVES 2

2 large Yukon Gold potatoes, about 20 oz (600 g) total, scrubbed
2 cups (500 mL) clarified butter
2 egg yolks
1 tbsp (15 mL) gastrique (page 234)
½ tsp (2 mL) lemon juice

3 drops each Tabasco and Worcestershire sauce
Pinch each of salt and white pepper
1 tbsp (15 mL) chopped tarragon
1 live lobster, about 1¼ lb (625 g), par-cooked and shelled (page 237), tail shell reserved
1 tbsp (15 mL) chopped chives

Par-cook the French fries according to the directions on page 194.

Lobster basket (optional): Preheat oven to 400°F (200°C). With sharp kitchen shears, trim away and discard the semi-translucent underside of the tail shell, then cut the hard shell in half lengthwise. Rinse well and shake dry. Puncture a hole in each shell half near the broad top of the tail and then through its tail fan. Arrange the two halves side by side with their tail fans pointing in opposite directions, the split top of the shell facing outward and what used to be its underside touching at centre. Make it circular by joining the two shell sections together end to end, bending them one at a time so that tail fan overlaps the adjoining tail base and the holes line up. Tie them together, then repeat at the second join. Place the basket on a baking sheet, brush with some of the butter, and roast until dry and fragrant—about 10 minutes.

Heat half the butter to 120°F (50°C). Place a stainless steel bowl over a pot of simmering water, add the egg yolks and gastrique, and whisk until the mixture thickens and turns pale yellow. Remove bowl from heat, and while whisking continuously, slowly add the warm butter. Stir in lemon juice, Tabasco, Worcestershire, salt, pepper, and tarragon and set the béarnaise aside in a warm place.

Heat the remaining butter to 170°F (75°C). Cut the lobster meat into bite-size pieces and add to the butter to heat through.

Finish cooking the French fries, then drain and toss with salt.

Place the lobster basket at the centre of a warm plate—or simply scatter the plate lightly with some of the chives. Add half the fries, then scatter half the butter-poached lobster and dabs of béarnaise on top. Make another layer, finishing with a generous smattering of béarnaise, and finally the remaining chives.

Optional: If the lobster is female, sauté the roe and sprinkle it over the poutine along with the chives.

Suggested wine: creamy Chardonnay or Champagne

Sandwiches

John Montagu, the 4th Earl of Sandwich (1718–92), had a habit of spending entire days at the card tables without ever breaking for a proper meal, getting by instead only on a steady supply of a little meat packaged between slices of bread, which is how the snack got its name. The sandwiches in this section, largely taken from the repertoire at Bymark, our restaurant in Toronto's financial district, suggest that it is hungrier work to gamble on stocks than cards. Each of them is a full meal in itself, and then some.

For some we took inspiration from American classics and applied a luxurious touch or two to raise them to a new standard. Others are inventions of our own. All of them are simple to prepare and completely satisfying. This is ideal weekend luncheon fare for everyone.

Meatloaf Panini

If meatloaf has a bad name, it must be a result of abuse of the bread crumb as filler. Here we use only a modicum of it for binding purposes, and the rest is all about top-quality meat and flavour enhancement. Properly prepared, this loaf is moist, tender, and enticingly toothsome. Slipping a couple of slices into a crisp panini was something we came up for the takeout counter in the early days at McEwan Fine Foods, where it remains a customer (and staff) favourite. **MAKES 1 MEATLOAF, ENOUGH FOR 10 PANINI**

4 tbsp (60 mL) canola oil
2 Spanish onions—1 diced, 1 sliced
1 cup (250 mL) barbecue sauce (page 225)
1½ lb (675 g) ground veal
1½ lb (675 g) lean ground beef
3 tbsp (45 mL) minced Italian parsley
1½ tbsp (23 mL) minced chives
1 tbsp (15 mL) minced thyme
3 tbsp (45 mL) MCO (or Heinz) chili sauce
1 tbsp (15 mL) Keen's dry mustard

1 cup (250 mL) panko bread crumbs
3 large eggs, beaten
Salt and white pepper

PANINI (PER SANDWICH)
1 panini roll
3 tbsp (45 mL) barbecue sauce (page 225)
2 thin slices medium cheddar
2 slices (about ½ inch/1 cm thick) meatloaf
3 tbsp (45 mL) caramelized sliced onions

MEATLOAF: Divide the oil between two large skillets and over low heat caramelize each onion separately. Set aside to cool. Preheat oven to 350°F (180°C).

Reserve ¼ cup (50 mL) of the barbecue sauce. Then put all the remaining meatloaf ingredients in a large bowl. Add 1 cup (250 mL) of caramelized diced onion and mix thoroughly. If the mixture is too wet (and sticks to clean hands), add more bread crumbs. If it is too dry (and crumbles easily when shaped), add more barbecue sauce. To test seasoning, remove a small, meatball-sized portion and fry it in a little oil in a hot skillet. Taste and adjust seasonings if necessary.

Line a large baking sheet with parchment paper. Transfer the mixture to the sheet and shape it into a tapered oblong resembling a loaf of rye bread. Poke it gently along its crest from one end to the other to create a shallow ridge. Fill this with the reserved barbecue sauce. Bake for about 1 hour, until the internal temperature is 165°F (72°C). Set aside to rest for at least 30 minutes before slicing.

PANINI: Slather the bottom of a panini bun with the barbecue sauce and then add one slice of the cheese, both slices of meatloaf, another slice of cheese, the sliced onions, and finally the top of the bun. Heat in a panini press until crisp.

Substitutions: If desired, use the best available quality of store-bought barbecue sauce. If panko is unavailable, regular dry bread crumbs will do.

Suggested wine: modern Chianti or Super Tuscan

Bymark Burgers

When in 2003 the great French chef Daniel Boulud challenged the "21" Club's long and uncontested reign as purveyors of the priciest burger in Manhattan with his own $29 dbBistro burger, there swiftly ensued a period of culinary one-upmanship now known as the Burger Wars. The reverberations quickly reached Toronto, where the very finest local super-burger was universally acknowledged to be this one from Bymark, where it remains a bestseller to this day. SERVES 4

2 lb (1 kg) Prime-grade strip loin
    (preferably USDA), untrimmed
2 tbsp (30 mL) olive oil
Salt and coarsely ground pepper
2 large king oyster mushrooms, sliced
2 tbsp (30 mL) butter
4 top-quality hamburger buns

1 cup (250 mL) truffle aïoli (page 222)
8 leaves red lettuce, preferably lolla rossa
7 oz (200 g) aged Brie de Meaux, sliced

OPTIONAL
¼ oz (8 g) black or summer truffle shavings
truffle oil
4 slices (each 2 oz/60 g) of fresh foie gras, seared

SUGGESTED ACCOMPANIMENT: Perfect French fries (page 194) or tempura-battered onion rings (page 200)

Trim (or ask your butcher to trim) the strip loin of any silverskin or connective tissue, and then pass it through a meat grinder fitted with a medium blade. Divide into four portions and then, slapping each portion from hand to hand with a twisting motion, form it into thick patties. Refrigerate for at least 1 hour.

Preheat grill on high.

Rub burgers with the olive oil and then encrust them with salt and pepper. Lightly oil the grill rack, sear the burgers well on both sides, and then relocate them to the more temperate side of the grill until they attain the preferred level of doneness—about 8 to 10 minutes for medium-rare.

Meanwhile, sauté the mushrooms in half the butter until they have softened, then mark (or crosshatch) them on the grill. Grill the buns and butter them lightly. Spread about 1 tbsp (15 mL) aïoli on the bottom of each bun. Add lettuce, then the burgers, cheese, mushrooms—and the optional truffle shavings or a few drops of truffle oil. Top burgers with bun tops and allow to rest for 6 or 7 minutes. If you are using foie gras, add it immediately before serving. Serve with chosen accompaniment and a ramekin of truffle aïoli.

Substitutions: The king oyster can be replaced with any good mushrooms—porcini are ideal.

Tip: Mini burger patties require 2 oz (60 g) beef each.

Suggested wine: Napa Cabernet

Brisket Sandwich

Everyone loves a brisket sandwich. Whether it's full of Montreal smoked meat or Texas BBQ or something in between, all that really matters is that the meat be the main event and that there be lots of it. Vegetables should never be tucked in there with it, taking up valuable space between the slices of soft bread. The supporting role falls exclusively to the sauce, which like mustard or barbecue sauce invariably packs an acidic counterpoint to the fat of the meat. Here we go with bright contrast from horseradish and herb tapenade. PER SANDWICH

2 slices of focaccia or 1 length of baguette, about 7 in (18 cm)
1 tsp (5 mL) or more herb tapenade (page 235)
At least 6 oz (175 g) leftover slow-braised brisket (page 139), sliced
Grated fresh horseradish
Reheated brisket gravy (page 139) for dipping

SUGGESTED ACCOMPANIMENTS: French fries (page 194), tempura-battered onion rings (page 200)

Slather bread with tapenade, follow with a mound of brisket, and grate the horseradish overtop. Close the sandwich and tuck in!

Suggested wine: Côtes du Rhône or Australian GSM blend

Pulled Pork Sandwich

We came up with this sandwich for Bymark as a way to cope with the inevitable leftovers when we'd cooked a 15-pound pork shoulder or 25-pound pork leg for dinner service the night before. We shred the meat, gently reheat it in its gravy, and then stuff it into a split Yorkshire pudding for a sublime result. What works so well at lunchtime in the restaurant is just as good a solution for leftover pork at home. **MAKES 8 TO 12 YORKSHIRE PUDDINGS**

1¼ cups (300 mL) whole milk
¼ cup (50 mL) cooked sweet corn kernels
4 eggs
1 cup (250 mL) flour, sifted
2 tbsp (30 mL) chopped chives
Pinch each of salt and white pepper
½ cup (125 mL) duck fat

PER SANDWICH
Leftover roast pork and its gravy
1 tsp (5 mL) herb tapenade (page 235)
About 2 tbsp (30 mL) Riesling apple sauce (page 227)

Preheat oven to 425°F (220°C).

Combine the milk and corn in a blender and whiz until smooth. Transfer to a bowl with the eggs and beat lightly with a whisk. Add the flour, chives, salt and pepper and whisk until well combined. Add 1 tbsp (15 mL) of the duck fat to each cup of a muffin pan and transfer to the oven. When the fat begins to smoke lightly, remove the pan to a work surface and add about ⅓ cup (75 mL) of batter to each muffin cup. Return the pan swiftly to the oven. After 5 minutes reduce the heat to 350°F (180°C). Cook until brown and crisp—about 15 minutes more.

To finish the sandwiches, shred leftover pork and reheat it in its gravy. Split the Yorkshire puddings top down, without cutting all the way through the bottom. Fill the pudding with the pulled pork, top with extra gravy, sprinkle with herb tapenade and serve with apple sauce on the side.

Suggested wine: Australian Grenache or juicy Spanish red

Lobster Grilled Cheese Sandwich

At Bymark we build this ultimate grilled cheese sandwich on the flavourful foundation of a rosemary focaccia from our local bakery Ace. Their focaccia is large, allowing for slices about 6 inches (15 cm) long and 2½ to 3 inches (6 to 9 cm) high, but you can of course use a more typical, smaller loaf—or a different bread altogether. If so, seek out a white bread of quality with a nicely aerated crumb, and consider sprinkling a little finely minced fresh rosemary on the buttered exterior before frying, a trick that goes some long way to replicating focaccia. SERVES 2

1 live lobster, about 1½ lb (750 g)
4 cups (1 L) court bouillon (page 246)
6 oz (175 g) aged Brie de Meaux, cold
4 slices focaccia, at least ¾ in (2 cm) thick
¼ cup (50 mL) soft butter
6 to 8 slices crisp pancetta (page 231)
6 tbsp (90 mL) lemon-garlic aïoli (page 223)

SUGGESTED ACCOMPANIMENTS: Pear and endive salad (page 240) with lemon-garlic vinaigrette (page 250), Perfect French fries (page 194), tempura-battered onion rings (page 200)

Preheat oven to 325°F (160°C).

Bring a large pot of salted water to a vigorous boil, plunge lobster into the pot head first, reduce heat, cover, and simmer for 7 minutes. Remove lobster, cool under running cold water, and drain. Shell the lobster and reserve the intentionally undercooked meat in the refrigerator.

Bring court bouillon to a bare simmer. Cut the Brie into slices ¼ inch (5 mm) thick. Slather one side of each focaccia slice generously with butter, and line them up buttered side down in a large nonstick skillet on medium-low heat. Cook the lobster in the court bouillon for 60 seconds—or until warmed through—and then drain it on paper towels. Divide the cheese among the four slices of bread, spacing it evenly. Top two of the slices with a row of three or four pancetta slices. Cut the lobster into large bite-size pieces and distribute it over the pancetta. Finally, flip the two cheese-covered focaccia slices onto the lobster side to complete the sandwiches.

Because of the thickness of the bread, the sandwiches should be flipped frequently—every minute or so. Add more butter to the pan as needed. When both sides are bronzed and the Brie is conspicuously melting, remove the sandwiches to a cutting board, slice them in half on a diagonal, and plate with a ramekin of aïoli and the selected accompaniment.

Suggested wine: a rich Chardonnay

Pasta and Risotto

For this section we assembled a list of favourites from the restaurants and in the process ended up with a selection of exceptional range. Some of these dishes are of the most rustic simplicity, perfect for a casual family meal. Others are highly refined. None is better than another. It all comes down to what you're in the mood for.

But there is a corollary benefit to mastering these dishes. For together they contain all the fundamentals of constructing a pasta dish that is exuberant with flavour, of building a risotto as a great side dish or a course all its own, and of making a gnocchi light enough for a summer luncheon or sufficiently rich to satisfy the heartiest appetite on a cold winter night. A handful of fresh peas, some stock or cream, a little leftover rabbit or lamb from the night before, the overripe tomatoes on the counter—all will suddenly fit into a new master plan for dinner.

Free-Form Lasagne with Prawns, Sweet Tomato, and Parsley

The long cooking time required for this tomato sauce produces results of exceptional sweetness, a quality echoed by that of the freshest, best quality shrimp. Avoid Asian Tiger and bland jumbo shrimp for this dish and aim instead to procure smaller, tastier, and more sensibly harvested white shrimp from Texas or the Caribbean—or best of all, in springtime, seek out B.C.'s incomparable spot prawns. SERVES 2 AS A STARTER

1 small batch pasta dough (page 239)
2 tbsp (30 mL) basic olive oil
¼ Spanish onion, thinly sliced
2 cloves garlic, smashed
1 can (28 oz/796 mL) San Marzano Roma
   tomatoes, drained
2 tsp (10 mL) granulated sugar
Salt and pepper
1 large sprig basil
1½ tbsp (30 mL) fine olive oil
2 tbsp (23 mL) minced onion or shallot
½ tsp (2 mL) minced garlic

8 large shrimp, peeled and deveined
2 tbsp (30 mL) white wine
2 tbsp (30 mL) minced parsley
2 tbsp (30 mL) whipped butter (page 251)
1 tbsp (15 mL) butter
1 tsp (5 mL) minced chives
1 tbsp (15 mL) grated Parmigiano-Reggiano
2 tbsp (30 mL) frothed butter sauce
   (optional; page 229)

GARNISH
2 basil leaves

Roll out the pasta as thinly as possible. Cut out 6 sheets, each about 3 inches by 4 inches (8 cm by 10 cm). Let them rest for 30 minutes, then boil them briefly and transfer to a baking sheet lubricated with a little of the basic olive oil. Sprinkle a little more oil over the pasta, and cover it tightly with plastic wrap. Set aside.

Heat 1 tbsp (15 mL) of the basic olive oil in a saucepan over medium heat, then cook the sliced onions and smashed garlic, stirring frequently, until translucent but not coloured. Add the tomatoes along with the sugar and a light seasoning of salt and pepper, then partially cover and, stirring periodically, simmer very gently for 90 minutes. Add the basil and simmer 5 minutes more. Discard the basil, add 1 tbsp (15 mL) fine olive oil, and stir well. Pass the sauce through the coarse disc of a food mill. It should be thick. Keep warm.

In a skillet over medium heat, cook the minced onion in the remaining 1 tbsp (15 mL) basic olive oil until it begins to wilt, then stir in minced garlic. After a minute, add the shrimp and cook lightly, then deglaze with white wine, leaving them underdone at the centre. Season.

Stir the parsley and whipped butter into the tomato sauce. Adjust seasonings, then add the shrimp. In a large skillet, melt the butter, then gently reheat the pasta with the chives. Place a sheet of pasta at the centre of two warm pasta plates. Top with one shrimp and some tomato sauce. Repeat. Add a third sheet, top with a pair of shrimp, some tomato sauce, a sprinkle of Parmesan, and, if you choose, a spoonful of butter sauce. Garnish with a basil leaf and a drizzle of the remaining fine olive oil.

Suggested wine: a bright, fruity Chardonnay or a soft, juicy young red

Butternut Squash Ravioli with Braised Oxtail

When the squash come out on display at your local farmers' market, you know that the time has come to bundle up for winter. A bittersweet moment—saved only by the arrival of the squash. No local variety is quite as useful as the butternut, which in addition to soup lends itself perfectly to filling ravioli. Here we pair them with a creamily rich ragù of oxtail to delicious effect. SERVES 6 AS AN APPETIZER OR 4 AS A MAIN COURSE

1 butternut squash, about 8 in/20 cm long, split
   lengthwise and seeded
1 tbsp (15 mL) olive oil
Pinch each of salt, pepper, and curry powder
2 cloves garlic, smashed
Vegetable oil for deep-frying
Pinch each of nutmeg, curry powder, salt, and pepper

1 batch pasta dough (page 239)
1 egg, lightly beaten
1 batch braised oxtail (page 228)
3 tbsp (45 mL) whipped butter (page 251)
2 tbsp (30 mL) fine olive oil
12 crispy sage leaves (page 180)

Preheat oven to 450°F (230°C).

Cut off the top 2 to 3 inches (5 to 8 cm) of each half of the squash and reserve. Place the squash halves flesh side up in a roasting pan and dress each with olive oil, salt, pepper, and curry powder, then put a garlic clove in each cavity. Cover with foil and roast for 30 minutes. Remove the foil and roast for another 45 minutes—or until tender.

Meanwhile, peel reserved squash and cut into ¼-inch (5 mm) dice. Fill a skillet at least 1½ inches (4 cm) deep with vegetable oil and heat it to 350°F (180°C). In batches if necessary, deep-fry squash until golden brown. Remove with a slotted spoon to drain on paper towels. Pass the roasted squash through a ricer into a large bowl. Add the deep-fried squash, nutmeg, and curry powder and fold until well mixed. Correct seasonings and set aside.

Roll the pasta into thin sheets and spread on a flour-dusted work surface. Use a 3- to 3½-inch (8 to 9 cm) circular cutter to cut pasta into discs. With a 1-inch (2.5 cm) melon baller, place a scoop of squash filling at the centre of half the pasta discs. Brush their edges with egg wash, place a second pasta disc on top of each one, and press the two pasta sheets together to seal while carefully pushing as much air from the ravioli as possible. Trim the ravioli with a 2½-inch (6 cm) cutter. Dust the ravioli lightly with flour and set aside.

To finish, reheat the braised oxtail. Boil 20-odd ravioli in salted water until they float—about 3 minutes. Taste the sauce, correct seasonings, turn off the heat, and stir in the butter. Mound a portion of the sauce in the centre of a warm pasta bowl and top with a circle of 3 (appetizer) to 5 (entrée) ravioli. Drizzle with fine olive oil and top with sage leaves.

Tip: Always cook more ravioli than you need because inevitably some will disintegrate in the boiling water. Steaming the ravioli is a little safer but takes a little longer. Be sure to brush the surface of the steaming basket with olive oil before placing the ravioli inside. A dab of butter on the surface of each is also a help.

Suggested wine: Grenache or New World Pinot Noir

Chestnut Ravioli with Seared Foie Gras and Madeira-Macerated Raisins

Foie gras always plays nicely with fruit and wine. And adding chestnut to the mix is hardly radical. But in this particular arrangement, these familiar flavours give the joyous impression of having just broken out together in an exuberant new song. The dish is a modern classic from One. SERVES 6 AS AN APPETIZER OR 4 AS A MAIN COURSE

1 cup (250 mL) golden raisins
1 cup (250 mL) Madeira
½ cup (125 mL) hot water
3 tbsp (45 mL) chopped onion
1 tbsp (15 mL) olive oil
½ cup (125 mL) diced Granny Smith apple
2 tsp (10 mL) granulated sugar
½ cup (125 mL) dry Riesling
Pinch each of ground cloves, cinnamon, and nutmeg

¼ cup (50 mL) 35% cream
2 cups (500 mL) pure chestnut paste
1 batch pasta dough (page 239)
1 egg, lightly beaten
12 oz (375 g) best-quality fresh foie gras
Salt
3 tbsp (45 mL) butter
1 tbsp (15 mL) minced chives
12 crispy sage leaves (page 180)

Combine the raisins, Madeira, and water in a bowl and leave raisins to soak for 2 hours. Drain raisins, reserving the soaking liquid. Transfer a quarter of the raisins and a quarter of the soaking liquid to a blender or food processor and purée. Reserve all three components separately.

In a sauté pan over medium heat, cook the onions in the oil until translucent. Stir in the apple, and 2 minutes later, the sugar. Cook until the apple is soft, and then deglaze with the Riesling. Add seasonings and cream, and reduce until it thickens. Stir in the chestnut paste. Heat through, then set aside to cool. Transfer to a food processor and pulse thoroughly. The mixture should be thick enough to hold its shape. Make chestnut ravioli as described for butternut squash ravioli on page 98.

Cut foie gras into 2-oz (60 g) slices for appetizers or 3-oz (85 g) slices for entrées. Score one side of each slice and salt generously. Sear in a hot, dry skillet for about 60 seconds per side. Transfer seared foie gras to a warm plate. Drain off almost all the fat from the pan and then add ½ cup (125 mL) of the raisin soaking liquid, ¼ cup (50 mL) of the macerated raisins, and 1 heaping tablespoon (25 mL) of the raisin paste. Reduce by about half over medium-high heat, and then emulsify with 1 tbsp (15 mL) of the butter. Correct seasonings.

Meanwhile, boil 20-odd ravioli in salted water until they float—about 3 minutes. Toss the drained ravioli with the remaining 2 tbsp (30 mL) butter and the chives, and then transfer to warmed serving bowls (3 per serving for an appetizer and 5 for an entrée). Pour the pan sauce over the ravioli. Top with seared foie gras and crispy sage.

Tip: If you want to use fresh chestnuts and purée them yourself after cooking and peeling them, soak them in white wine for 3 minutes before transferring them to the food processor.

Suggested wine: Barolo or a high-toned Pinot Noir

Pappardelle with Braised Rabbit, Lardons, and Peas

This pasta dish has substance, but lightness too, as it is built on lean rabbit and stock and brightened with peas. That makes it a perfect dish for a cool early-summer evening. And as most of the work can be done well ahead of time, it makes a perfect meal for the first night of a cottage weekend. **SERVES 6 AS AN APPETIZER OR 4 AS A MAIN COURSE**

1 rabbit, about 3½ lb (1.6 kg), cut into 6 serving pieces
Pappardelle
3 tbsp (45 mL) olive oil
½ cup (125 mL) chopped onion
2 tsp (10 mL) minced garlic
½ cup (125 mL) dry Riesling
1 cup (250 mL) sweet peas, blanched
½ cup (125 mL) slab bacon strips, fried until lightly crisped
Salt and pepper
2 tbsp (30 mL) minced parsley
3 tbsp (45 mL) whipped butter (page 251)
½ cup (125 mL) grated Pecorino Romano

Braise the rabbit as described on page 160 but omit the mustard. Allow to cool slightly, then strain, reserving 2 cups (500 mL) of the braising liquid. Shred the meat from the bone and set aside, tightly covered.

Cook the pasta, reserving ¼ cup (50 mL) cooking water.

While the pasta cooks, in a sauté pan cook the onion in olive oil until translucent. Stir in the garlic and cook a minute longer. Add the shredded rabbit and deglaze with wine. Add the rabbit braising liquid and reduce slightly. Add the peas and lardons. Season, then stir in the parsley. Add the pasta and reserved cooking water, and toss well. If dry, add more rabbit braising liquid. Remove from the heat, add the butter, and toss well. Serve topped with grated pecorino.

Suggested wine: Pouilly-Fumé or Chablis

Linguine with Shrimp, Chorizo, and Preserved Chilies

This rustic-minded pasta dish is loaded with flavour. Seafood and chorizo always swim nicely together. Chopped tomatoes, preserved chilies, and whipped butter elevate the excursion to something celebratory. SERVES 6 AS AN APPETIZER OR 4 AS A MAIN COURSE

Linguine
1 tbsp (15 mL) olive oil
12 large shrimp, shelled, deveined, and halved lengthwise
1 cured chorizo sausage, cut diagonally into ⅛-in (3 mm) slices
1 cooked chorizo sausage, cut diagonally into ⅛-in (3 mm) slices
¼ cup (50 mL) Italian soffritto (page 244)
2 tbsp (30 mL) chopped oil-preserved red chili
Tomato concassé (page 249), made with 4 Roma tomatoes
¼ cup (50 mL) chopped Italian parsley
¼ cup (50 mL) whipped butter (page 251)
Pinch each of salt and pepper

Cook the pasta, reserving ¼ cup (50 mL) cooking water.

While the pasta cooks, sauté the shrimp very briefly in olive oil over medium-high heat, just until pink all over. Add the cured and cooked chorizo, and once it is heated through stir in the soffritto and preserved chili. Combine with the linguine, and then add the tomato concassé and parsley. Toss well. Stir in whipped butter. If needed, lubricate the pasta further with a little of the reserved pasta cooking water. Correct seasonings.

Substitutions: Shelled lobster cut into bite-size pieces fits into the flavour profile of this dish just as nicely as shrimp. Two 1½-lb (750 g) lobsters will do generously.

Suggested wine: Rioja or Tuscan red

Rigatoni with Braised Lamb Shank

This combination of supple, flavoursome shank meat lightened with tomato and basil and spiked with chili makes for an exceptionally satisfying and robust pasta dish. SERVES 6 AS AN APPETIZER OR 4 AS A MAIN COURSE

LAMB
2 lamb shanks, about 1 lb (450 g) each
⅓ cup (75 mL) olive oil
Salt and pepper
½ cup (125 mL) each diced carrot, celery, and onion
1 bay leaf
4 sprigs thyme
2 sprigs rosemary
1 cup (250 mL) red wine
1 quart (1 L) white chicken stock (page 246)
1 tsp (5 mL) gastrique (page 234)

PASTA
Rigatoni
½ cup (125 mL) chopped onion
3 tbsp (45 mL) olive oil
2 tsp (10 mL) minced garlic
½ cup (125 mL) white wine
2 cups (500 mL) oil-preserved Italian cherry tomatoes, chopped
1 tbsp (15 mL) seeded and minced oil-preserved red chilies
2 tbsp (30 mL) basic tomato sauce (page 225)
1 cup (250 mL) torn basil leaves
½ cup (125 mL) minced parsley
3 tbsp (45 mL) whipped butter (page 251)
½ cup (125 mL) grated Pecorino Romano

LAMB: Preheat oven to 325°F (160°C). Sprinkle shanks with a little olive oil, season generously, and in a large ovenproof saucepan sear well in 2 tbsp (30 mL) of the oil until well browned on all sides. Remove lamb and pour off the oil from the saucepan. Add 2 tbsp (30 mL) fresh oil, and cook the diced vegetables with the bay leaf, thyme, and rosemary. When the vegetables begin to brown, return the lamb to the pot and deglaze with half the wine. Reduce completely and repeat with the remaining wine. Then add 1 cup (250 mL) of the stock, reduce by about a third, and add another cup. Repeat until all the stock is used and the lamb is virtually submerged. Cover the pot and transfer to the oven. Check for tenderness after 2 hours—and again if necessary every 20 minutes after that. The lamb should be soft and pulling away from the bone. When the shanks are done, remove them from the braising liquid to cool slightly. Discard the herbs and bay leaf and skim off the fat. Blitz the remaining liquid in a blender and then strain. Adjust the acidity by adding gastrique, and season with salt and pepper. Reserve 1 cup (250 mL) braising liquid. Strip lamb from the bones, shred, and set aside, covered.

Cook the pasta, reserving ½ cup (125 mL) cooking water.

While the pasta cooks, in a sauté pan cook the onion in olive oil until translucent. Add the garlic and cook a minute longer. Add the shredded lamb and deglaze with the wine. Add the reserved braising liquid, tomatoes, and chilies. Stir and heat through. Add tomato sauce, basil, and parsley and stir well. Add the pasta and half the reserved pasta water, and toss. Adjust seasonings. If the sauce is too thick, add more pasta water. Remove from the heat, add the butter, and toss again. Serve topped with grated pecorino.

Substitutions: This pasta is adaptable to all seasons. In summertime we use white wine in the braise for a lighter sauce; in the fall and winter we sometimes enrich the braising pot with tomato and saffron. If Italian cherry tomatoes are unavailable, use any sweet tomato of quality. Likewise, fresh or dried chilies can be used to provide heat in place of the preserved chilies.

Suggested wine: Washington State Cabernet or Super Tuscan

Spaghetti with Veal and Ricotta Meatballs

The key to a good meatball is in the texture: the goal is lightness, a lack of density. Here, veal and ricotta work together to achieve that without any compromise in flavour. You may cook the meatballs in the tomato sauce if you wish. But the meatballs are more succulent and flavourful and the sauce remains lighter if you cook the two separately and combine them just before serving. **SERVES 6**

½ Spanish onion, minced
1 cup (250 mL) olive oil
1 tbsp (15 mL) minced garlic
2 lb (1 kg) ground veal
2 cups (500 mL) ricotta cheese
3 egg whites
⅔ cup (150 mL) grated Parmigiano-Reggiano
½ cup (125 mL) minced Italian parsley
½ bunch chives, minced

2 tbsp (30 mL) minced oregano
1 tbsp (15 mL) minced thyme
Salt and pepper
Spaghetti for 6
2 batches basic tomato sauce (page 225)
2 cups (500 mL) basil leaves, torn
4 tbsp (60 mL) whipped butter (page 251)
Grated Parmigiano-Reggiano to taste

In a heavy-bottomed skillet, sweat the onions in 2 tbsp (30 mL) of the oil until translucent. Add the garlic, sweat a minute longer, and then cool the mixture in the refrigerator. In a large bowl combine the veal, ricotta, egg whites, Parmesan, parsley, chives, oregano, thyme, and the cooled onion and garlic; season generously. Work it all together well with your hands for at least 5 minutes. Remove a small portion and fry it in hot oil. Taste and adjust seasonings if necessary.

Rinse hands under cold running water and begin forming meatballs of desired size, rinsing hands again as necessary whenever the meat gets sticky. Collect meatballs on a baking sheet. Dust them with flour. Heat one or two large skillets on medium-high, heat the remaining oil, and sear the meatballs in batches if necessary, browning them nicely on all sides before setting them aside to drain on paper towels.

Cook the spaghetti, reserving some of the cooking water.

While the pasta cooks, heat the tomato sauce, then add the meatballs and torn basil. Add the desired amount to the drained pasta. Fold to combine, add a little pasta water to lubricate if needed, and fold in the butter. Serve topped off with extra sauce and Parmesan to taste.

Suggested wine: Chianti

Fried Gnocchi with Gorgonzola Cream Sauce and Woodland Mushrooms

The flavours at play here are basic. But in elevating the fried potato to the form of gnocchi, letting cheese speak in the pungent full-bodied voice of Gorgonzola, and hitting the earthy mushroom notes with the exquisite chanterelle, a familiar combination of flavours attains its apotheosis. SERVES 6 AS AN APPETIZER OR 4 AS A MAIN COURSE

GNOCCHI
2 tbsp (30 mL) clarified butter
1 batch (about 50 pieces) jalapeño gnocchi (page 235)

WOODLAND MUSHROOMS
1 tbsp (15 mL) olive oil
1 tbsp (15 mL) butter
2 tbsp (30 mL) minced onion
8 oz (225 g) chanterelles, larger ones sliced
1 tsp (5 mL) minced garlic
Pinch each of salt and white pepper
2 tbsp (30 mL) white wine
1 tsp (5 mL) combined minced parsley, rosemary, and sage

GORGONZOLA CREAM SAUCE
2 tbsp (30 mL) olive oil
¼ cup (50 mL) minced onion
2 tsp (10 mL) minced garlic
½ cup (125 mL) white wine
2 cups (500 mL) 35% cream
Pinch each of salt and white pepper
2 oz (60 g) Gorgonzola
1 tbsp (15 mL) minced chives

GARNISH
1 tbsp (15 mL) chive oil (page 232)
Fresh herb sprouts or sprigs of chervil

GNOCCHI: Thoroughly heat two large nonstick skillets over medium heat and lubricate them well with clarified butter. Divide the gnocchi evenly between them and fry until they brown on one side, then turn and repeat. Remove from the heat and set aside, keeping warm.

WOODLAND MUSHROOMS: Gently clean the mushrooms with a brush or a damp cloth. Heat the oil in a large skillet over medium-high heat. Add the butter, and when it foams add the onions and mushrooms. When the mushrooms begin to soften, stir in the garlic. Season with salt and pepper. One minute later, deglaze with the wine, then add the herbs. Remove from the heat and cover loosely to keep warm.

GORGONZOLA CREAM SAUCE: Heat the oil in a deep saucepan and sauté the onions until they wilt—4 to 5 minutes. Add the garlic, cook a minute further, and then deglaze with the wine. When the liquid becomes syrupy, stir in the cream. When it begins to simmer, season lightly and then crumble the Gorgonzola into the sauce. Stir until the cheese is incorporated, then add the chives and correct seasonings. Do not reduce.

Evenly distribute the gnocchi among warm pasta bowls, clustering them at the centre. Pour the sauce around and over the gnocchi—but do not douse them. Mound the chanterelles carefully over the top, garnish each bowl with a judicious sprinkling of chive oil and a light scattering of herbs, and serve at once.

Substitutions: Nearly any blue cheese of quality, from Danish blue to Roquefort to bleu de St-Benoit, will work with this dish. Other seasonal mushrooms, such as morels, lobster mushrooms, and bluefoot, work nicely too.

Suggested wine: Amarone or a rich Cabernet

Gnocchi with Summer Tomato Sauce

This tomato sauce is, like all the best of them, simple to execute. And as long as you make it from the best available ingredients, the pleasure the dish yields will far exceed the small effort required to put it together. The sauce is the ideal solution for once great tomatoes that have ripened past prime. Pairing it with good gnocchi takes it a few steps further.
SERVES 6 AS AN APPETIZER OR 4 AS A MAIN COURSE

3 lb (1.5 kg) very ripe (but not mealy) heirloom tomatoes
3 tbsp (45 mL) olive oil
½ cup (125 mL) minced onion
1 tsp (5 mL) minced garlic
½ cup (125 mL) white wine
1 batch gnocchi (page 235)
2 cups basil leaves, torn
Salt and pepper
4 tbsp (60 mL) whipped butter (page 251)
1 cup (250 mL) grated Parmigiano-Reggiano or Pecorino Romano

Cut a shallow X in the bottom of each tomato, then blanch the tomatoes for 60 seconds, shock them in ice water, and peel. Quarter them and remove and discard the core and seeds. Set aside.

In a sauté pan, cook the onion in the olive oil over medium heat until it becomes translucent. Stir in the garlic, and a minute later deglaze with the wine. When that is reduced to virtually nothing, add the tomatoes. Simmer for no more than 7 minutes, breaking their flesh apart with a wooden spoon as they cook. Add torn basil and season lightly.

Meanwhile, cook the gnocchi. Using a spider or slotted spoon, transfer the gnocchi to the pan with the sauce. Toss, and correct seasonings. Stir in the butter, and serve generously topped with grated cheese.

Suggested wine: a fresh Italian white or young Chianti or Valpolicella

Risotto with Peas, Bacon, and Foie Gras

There are a few important things to know about risotto. First off, do not be intimidated by it: a good risotto requires patience and attentiveness but no great culinary skill. Second, the idea that a risotto must be stirred almost continuously is incorrect—doing so will yield an excessively starchy, gluey result. Stirring regularly, but not obsessively, yields the best dish. So too does Carnaroli rice, the only kind used in McEwan restaurants. Vialone Nano is in our opinion a close second, and Arborio a distant third. **SERVES 4 AS AN APPETIZER**

3 tbsp (45 mL) olive oil
1 cup (250 mL) minced onion
Salt
1 tsp (5 mL) minced garlic
1¼ cups (300 mL) Carnaroli rice
½ cup (125 mL) white wine
1 quart (1 L) white chicken stock (page 246), at a simmer
4 oz (125 g) top-quality lightly smoked bacon, diced
½ cup (125 mL) sweet peas, blanched

½ cup (125 mL) freshly grated Parmigiano-Reggiano
3 tbsp (45 mL) 35% cream
2 tbsp (30 mL) foie gras mousse (or a 4-oz/125 g slice of fresh foie gras, seared and chopped)
2 tbsp (30 mL) truffle paste (optional)
1 tbsp (15 mL) butter
Ground white pepper
4 slices crisp pancetta (optional; page 231)

Heat 2 tbsp (30 mL) of the oil in a heavy-bottomed pot over medium heat. Add the onions, salt lightly, and sweat, stirring frequently so the onions do not brown. When after 5 or 6 minutes the onions begin to wilt, add the garlic and cook a minute longer. Add the rice and stir well to coat with the oil. Add more oil if necessary. Continue cooking, stirring frequently, until the grains of rice begin to acquire translucence (if uncertain, lift a few grains from the pot and examine them against the dark backdrop of your wooden spoon). When that is achieved, deglaze with the wine.

When the wine has been reduced to virtual syrup, add ½ cup (125 mL) of the hot stock. Stir again. When the liquid once again thickens, add ¼ cup (50 mL) stock and stir again. Season lightly. Stir regularly, and build the seasoning gradually as you go. Continue until the rice is nearly cooked and the stock nearly finished.

Meanwhile, cook the bacon until barely crisp at the edges; drain on paper towels. Stir the bacon into the risotto, followed by the peas and cheese. Heat through. Remove pot from heat. Stir in the cream, foie gras mousse, optional truffle paste, and butter. Taste and correct seasonings with salt and white pepper. If desired, finish on the plate with shards of crisp pancetta.

Tip: It is not true that risotto must be cooked right through from start to finish; cooking it until 5 minutes shy of completion, chilling it quickly, and resuming the preparation later on has no discernible effect on the taste or texture of the rice. To cool it quickly, spread the par-cooked rice on a baking sheet and refrigerate immediately. This is what restaurants do—and especially the ones that announce grandly on their menu "N.B.: risotto takes 20 minutes to prepare."

Suggested wine: a rich, full-bodied white, like a smoky Chardonnay

Risotto with Sweet Peas and Lake Erie Yellow Perch Fillets

The sustainably fished Lake Erie yellow perch has a firm, mildly sweet flesh, as well as a tasty thin skin that lends itself nicely to crisping up in a hot pan. Both those virtues combine most harmoniously with creamy risotto and spring peas. Any fish of similar qualities will work as a stand-in. **SERVES 4 AS AN APPETIZER**

1 batch risotto (page 111)
8 Lake Erie yellow perch fillets, about 2 oz (60 g) each
1 tbsp (15 mL) olive oil
1 tsp (5 mL) salt
1 tbsp (15 mL) vegetable oil
2 tbsp (30 mL) butter
½ cup (125 mL) frothed butter sauce (optional; page 229)

GARNISH
Sprigs of chervil or minced chives

Begin cooking the risotto according to the directions on page 111, but omit the foie gras and bacon.

When the risotto is nearly done, pat the perch fillets dry with paper towels. Rub them lightly with olive oil and sprinkle with salt. Heat a large nonstick skillet on medium-high and add the vegetable oil and butter. When the butter has stopped foaming, add the fillets skin side down and immediately place a slightly smaller skillet over them to prevent curling. After about 2 minutes, remove the top skillet, flip the fish, and cook—uncovered—until done, about 2 minutes more. Transfer the fish to a warm plate.

Finish the risotto. Plate individually or on a serving platter, topping the risotto with perch fillets arranged skin side up. Finish with butter sauce, if desired, and the garnish.

Substitutions: Pickerel fillets (pictured) cut into small portions work just as nicely in this dish as the perch. And looking beyond local sources, red mullet is a superb and prettily coloured alternative.

Suggested wine: crisp Soave

Fish and Shellfish

My experience suggests that we do not cook nearly enough fish at home—not in Toronto, anyway. We sell far more fish by proportion in the restaurants than we do raw product at McEwan Fine Foods. What customers do like to buy from the fish counter there are semi-prepared products, like halibut in banana leaf with aromatics, or miso-glazed cod, all tidily packaged and ready to pop in the oven. Local home cooks are apparently more at ease working with meat and poultry. This is a mystery to me.

So to make fish a little less mysterious to you, I have included the recipes for those perennially popular halibut and cod dishes. The balance of the recipes runs the gamut from dead simple to slightly challenging. You will see that many of the recipes include a suggestion for an optional sauce that at the restaurants we refer to by the very honest moniker of "butter sauce." Do make it: there is not a fish in the ocean that it does not enhance upon contact.

Halibut with Braised Tomato, Fingerling Potatoes, Celery, and Olives

From the point of view of the halibut, one might say that the fish is too versatile in the kitchen for its own good. Here we dress it up with a long-stewed sweet tomato sauce enhanced with celery and olives. The dish is light but eminently satisfying in summer or winter. SERVES 4

7 Roma tomatoes, blanched and peeled
½ large Spanish onion, thinly sliced
¼ cup (50 mL) olive oil
2 tbsp (30 mL) chopped garlic
½ cup (125 mL) white wine
7 canned San Marzano Roma tomatoes, cored
    and crushed
Salt and pepper
12 fingerling potatoes, peeled

1 celery stalk
4 skinless halibut fillets, about 6 oz (175 g) each
2 tbsp (30 mL) butter
12 pitted black olives, halved
Leaves from ¼ bunch cilantro, chopped
2 tbsp (30 mL) whipped butter (page 251)
¼ cup (50 mL) frothed butter sauce
    (optional; page 229)
4 basil leaves

Preheat oven to 400°F (200°C).

Remove the tops from the peeled tomatoes, quarter them, and halve each quarter lengthwise. Set aside. In a sauté pan over medium heat, cook the onions in half the olive oil. After they begin to wilt, add the garlic. A few minutes later, raise the heat and deglaze with the wine. As soon as the wine has evaporated, add the fresh tomatoes to the pan and sauté for a few minutes. Then add the canned tomatoes. Season lightly, and simmer, uncovered, for 45 minutes, stirring frequently and adjusting the seasoning periodically as you go.

Meanwhile, simmer or steam the potatoes until fork-tender; set aside. With a vegetable peeler shave the fibrous exterior from the celery stalk, then cut it into four equal lengths. Divide each of those lengthwise into four batonets. Blanch in salted water until tender and then shock in ice water.

Massage the halibut fillets with a little olive oil and season them. Heat an ovenproof skillet on medium-high, add the remaining olive oil, and sear the fillets skin side up until bronzed—4 to 5 minutes. Turn the fillets, add 1 tbsp (15 mL) of butter, and transfer the pan to the oven. Roast until the fish is just cooked through—another 6 to 10 minutes, depending on thickness.

To finish the tomato sauce, stir in the olives and cilantro, and then stir in the whipped butter. Taste and adjust seasonings. Reheat the celery and potatoes in the remaining 1 tbsp (15 mL) butter. Spoon about 3 tbsp (45 mL) of the tomato sauce onto four warmed plates. Divide the celery and potatoes among them, placing them on top of the sauce. Follow with a fillet of fish, 1 tbsp (15 mL) of butter sauce if desired, and a basil leaf for garnish.

Suggested wine: Loire white or a light Mediterranean red

Crispy Prosciutto-Wrapped Sea Bass with Lentils

Here the prosciutto serves to keep the fish exceptionally moist as well as provide it with a skin more toothsome than that which nature provided. The layer of paper-thin crispy pork is reminiscent of bacon in some ways, and as very few flavours fit together more naturally than pork and beans, it helps link fish to lentils in this splendid dish. SERVES 2

1 tbsp (15 mL) minced onion
2 tbsp (30 mL) olive oil
½ tsp (2 mL) minced garlic
¾ cup (175 mL) beluga or Puy lentils, picked over
2 cups (500 mL) white chicken stock (page 246)
2 skinless striped sea bass fillets, about 6 oz (175 g) each
Pinch each of salt and white pepper
4 thin slices prosciutto di Parma
1 tbsp (15 mL) butter
2 tbsp (30 mL) Italian soffritto (page 244)
1 whole scallion, thinly sliced diagonally

2 tbsp (30 mL) tomato concassé (page 249)
2 tbsp (30 mL) finely chopped parsley
3 tbsp (45 mL) whipped butter (page 251)
2 generous dashes each Tabasco and Worcestershire sauce
2 tbsp (30 mL) lemon juice
1 tbsp (15 mL) capers, rinsed and dried
Salt and pepper

GARNISH
Chopped chives
Micro greens

Preheat oven to 375°F (190°C).

Sweat the onion in half of the olive oil until it begins to wilt. Add the garlic and cook a minute longer. Stir in the lentils and chicken stock, bring to a simmer, and then cover. Cook until just tender—20 to 30 minutes.

Meanwhile, cut each fillet of fish in half crosswise and season lightly on all sides. Arrange slices of prosciutto in two overlapping sets, stack a pair of fish fillets on top of each—skin side out and thickest part against thinnest to ensure even cooking—and then roll them into neat packages. Heat an ovenproof skillet over medium heat and melt the butter in the remaining olive oil. Cook the fish on one side until the prosciutto is crisp and beginning to brown—2 to 3 minutes. Then flip the two parcels, cook for a minute longer, and transfer the skillet to the oven to finish cooking—about 10 minutes. It should feel firm to the touch when done. Set the fish aside to rest.

Reheat the lentils. They should be moist but not soupy, so drain off any liquid if necessary. Stir in the soffritto, scallion, tomato, and parsley. Remove from the heat and fold in 1 tbsp (15 mL) of the whipped butter. Correct the seasonings, and then mound the lentils in the centre of two warm plates. Slice the bass parcels in two diagonally and prop the two halves against each other on top of the two portions of lentils. Return the skillet in which the fish was cooked to medium-high heat, add the Tabasco and Worcestershire sauces and lemon juice, and foam briefly. Remove from the heat and add the capers, remaining whipped butter, and a pinch of salt and pepper, swirl the pan well, and pour the emulsified sauce over the fish. Garnish and serve.

Tip: You may use ordinary butter in place of the whipped butter to make the sauce; the emulsification will not be the same, but the flavour components will otherwise all be there.

Suggested wine: light Portuguese red or New World Pinot Noir

Halibut Baked in Banana Leaf with Curry-Scented Coconut Milk, Roasted Onions, and Cilantro

In French cuisine, preparing a piece of fish *en papillote* means cooking it with herbs, wine, and other accompaniments sealed in a pouch of parchment paper, which is usually cut open at the table so as to maximize the appetite-enhancing effect of its escaping aromas. In places like the Philippines, Malaysia, and Singapore, there is a similar convention, but instead of using a wrapping of paper—which has no flavour to impart—they typically use the large leaf of the banana tree, which does. And that leaf is just one of an exquisite abundance of aromatic flavours at play in this lovely dish. SERVES 6

12 banana leaves
4 tbsp (60 mL) olive oil
6 halibut fillets, about 5 oz (150 g) each, preferably skinless
2 tbsp (30 mL) chopped parsley
¼ cup (50 mL) clarified butter
18 to 24 roasted sugar beets (page 189), halved
3 medium leeks, white part only, sliced ¼-in (5 mm) thick, steamed and cooled
18 to 24 saffron pearl onions (page 197)
1 orange
1 lemon
1 large piece lemongrass, cut into six ½-in (1 cm) discs, pounded with a hammer

18 sprigs cilantro
6 small sprigs thyme
6 small sprigs parsley
1 small ginger bulb, peeled and julienned
12 fresh Thai chilies, split and seeded
6 tbsp (90 mL) butter
1 can (12 oz/400 mL) coconut milk
Salt

DRY RUB
½ tbsp (7 mL) coriander seeds, toasted and crushed
½ tsp (2 mL) cracked black pepper
Pinch each of ground cumin, curry powder, and salt

ACCOMPANIMENTS: This fish and its richly flavoured coconut milk sauce are ideally suited to the simple accompaniment of some absorbent jasmine rice. But if you prefer an all-in-one approach, forgo the rice and instead include two par-boiled and halved fingerling potatoes along with the other vegetables nestled beneath the halibut in each package.

Preheat oven to 375°F (190°C).

With a very sharp knife carefully trim the rib from the edge of each banana leaf, cutting it off in as thin a strip as possible. Reserve (you will use it as string later). Then trim the other edges so as to shape each leaf into a 12-inch (30 cm) square. Moisten a paper towel with a little of the oil and wipe the leaves along the grain to give them a pleasant sheen. Stack the leaves in pairs arranged so that their grains run perpendicular.

Combine the ingredients for the dry rub and sprinkle it over the top of the fish fillets. Combine the remaining oil and the parsley in a platter or baking dish, then gently roll the fish fillets in it to coat. Heat the clarified butter in a large, heavy-bottomed nonstick skillet over medium-high heat. Add the fillets seasoned side down, quickly searing them until they acquire some colour. Return fillets uncooked side down to the dish with the oil and parsley and set aside.

At the centre of each set of banana leaves, arrange a small mélange of vegetables: beet halves (or segments if large), leek slices, and pearl onions. Place a fillet of fish on top, seared side up. Zest the lemon and orange overtop. Add a piece of lemongrass. Tie together six herb bundles, combining in each 3 sprigs of cilantro, 1 sprig each thyme and parsley, 6 batonets of ginger, and 2 chilies. Place one on top of each fillet. Top each package with 1 tbsp (15 mL) butter. Shake coconut milk well and pour about ¼ cup (50 mL) over each fish. Add a pinch of salt, then seal each package tightly, folding the leaf edges as if wrapping paper around a gift, and using the strapping as a ribbon to tie it shut.

Place the packages on a baking sheet and transfer to the oven. Cooking time varies considerably with the thickness of the fish. After about 20 minutes, insert a meat thermometer through the top of a package. The fish is done when the temperature reads 135°F (58°C). Cut the packages open at the table and remove the lemongrass and herb bundles.

Substitutions: Do not feel obliged to follow this recipe to the letter. If your local grocer is out of lemongrass, for example, you can leave it out and still end up with an enviably flavourful and moist piece of fish. You may substitute the saffron onions for pearl onions that have merely been blanched and roasted until tender. The same goes for the wrapping: if banana leaves are unavailable, parchment paper will do in a pinch. For a vegetarian option or side dish, replace the fish (and its dry rub) with potatoes, carrots, and other root vegetables.

Tip: This is an excellent make-ahead dish for a dinner party, as you can make the fish parcels up to a day in advance, leaving yourself little to do after the guests arrive except pop them in the oven and make some rice. Let the packages come to room temperature before baking.

Suggested wine: a rich, aromatic Viognier

Pan-Roasted John Dory with Butter-Poached Crab and Crispy Potatoes

John Dory is a magnificent but often underappreciated fish. Nowadays it is largely sourced from the waters off New Zealand, and so you'll likely need to give your fishmonger considerable advance notice. The species has an unusually large head, and so the two fillets requested here come from an entire 2½-lb (1.1 kg) fish. SERVES 2

1 Dungeness or snow crab, about 2 lb (1 kg)
1 batch court bouillon (page 246)
1 large Yukon Gold potato
2 oz (60 mL) dry vermouth
1 pound (450 g) cold butter, cubed
Juice of 1 lemon
Salt and pepper
2 tbsp (30 mL) olive oil

5 tbsp (75 mL) soft butter
2 skinless John Dory fillets, about 5 oz (150 g) each
Pinch of white pepper
2 spears each white and green asparagus, peeled and blanched
½ tsp (2 mL) minced chives
¼ cup (50 mL) butter sauce (page 229)

Simmer the crab in court bouillon for 10 minutes (you want it to be underdone). Remove, run under cold water to stop the cooking, and shell. Keep the claw meat intact, and do not forget to remove the flesh tucked behind the gills in the carapace; your total yield should be about 8 oz (250 g).

With the aid of a sharp vegetable peeler or a paring knife, whittle the potato down into a cylinder of about 1½ inches (4 cm) diameter. Cut it into slices ¼ inch (5 mm) thick. Parboil the discs in salted water, shock in ice water, and reserve the best half dozen.

Prepare a *beurre monté*, beginning by heating the vermouth in a saucepan and then incorporating the cold cubed butter piece by piece over low heat, whisking almost constantly. Then whisk in the lemon juice slowly so as not to break the emulsion. Season, and keep warm at a temperature between 160 and 180°F (70 and 83°C).

In a large skillet over medium heat, heat 1 tbsp (15 mL) of the oil and 2 tbsp (30 mL) of the butter. Season the fish fillets with salt and white pepper and fry them until golden—2 to 3 minutes on each side. Transfer the fish to the centre of two warm plates.

Meanwhile, add the reserved crabmeat to the *beurre monté*. In a small skillet heat the remaining oil and 2 tbsp (30 mL) of the soft butter over medium-high heat. Fry the potatoes until bronzed on both sides, and then season them well. Transfer to a plate. Wipe out the skillet, add 1 tbsp (15 mL) butter, and quickly revive the asparagus. Add chives and season.

Use a slotted spoon to retrieve the crab meat from the *beurre monté* and mound it on top of the fish, leaning a claw up against the smaller pieces of meat. Surround each fish fillet with 3 crisp potato discs. Halve the asparagus spears crosswise and distribute them between the potatoes, alternating colours. Froth the butter sauce and drizzle all around.

Substitutions: Another firm white fish can be used; halibut in particular loves the company of crab.

Shortcut: Instead of making butter sauce specifically for this dish, you can simply adjust the salt and pepper in the *beurre monté* used to heat the crab and use that instead. It may be frothed, too.

Suggested wine: aged white Burgundy or oak-aged Chardonnay

Dover Sole with Orange Segments, Hazelnuts, and Brown Butter

The firm-fleshed Dover sole is, along with the turbot, one of the finest flatfish of the North Sea. It loves the company of butter, and nuts too—in the familiar form of sole *amandine*. Here we have exchanged mild almonds for the more robust hazelnut and added the rich flavour of charred orange. SERVES 2

½ cup (125 mL) hazelnuts
1 medium navel orange
Flour for dredging
Salt and pepper
2 Dover sole, about 1 lb (450 g) each, cleaned, dark skin peeled but white skin left on
1 tbsp (15 mL) basic marinade (page 225)

¼ cup (50 mL) clarified butter
1 tbsp (15 mL) olive oil
3 tbsp (45 mL) butter
Dash each of Tabasco and Worcestershire
2 tsp (10 mL) freshly squeezed lemon juice
1 tsp (5 mL) combined chopped sage, thyme, and parsley
Crispy parsley (optional; page 180)

RECOMMENDED ACCOMPANIMENTS: Wilted spinach (page 180), braised chard (page 180), roasted sugar beets (page 189), sautéed chanterelles (page 179) with sweet peas, crispy potatoes

Preheat oven to 375°F (190°C). Spread hazelnuts on a baking sheet and roast for 7 or 8 minutes. Transfer them to a clean kitchen cloth and rub them together to remove their skins. Chop the cleaned nuts coarsely and set aside. Leave the oven on.

Preheat grill—or grill pan—on high. Cut the orange into slices about ½ inch (1 cm) thick. Sprinkle lightly with some of the olive oil and char quickly. When cool, cut out orange segments and set aside.

Combine the flour, salt, and pepper. Rub each cleaned sole with marinade and then dredge in the seasoned flour. In an ovenproof nonstick skillet large enough to accommodate both fish (or two smaller pans), heat the clarified butter and remaining olive oil over medium heat. Fry the fish white skin side down until the edges get brown and crisp—about 4 minutes. Flip the fish and transfer the pan to the oven until the fish is cooked through—about 12 minutes. Let fish rest 3 or 4 minutes, then fillet each one into three—the side with skin attached will become a double fillet. Plate the reassembled fish skin side up. Cover loosely with foil to keep warm.

To prepare brown butter, heat a skillet over high heat until it's very hot. Add the butter, scald for 15 seconds, and remove from the heat. Swirl in the Tabasco, Worcestershire, and lemon juice. Scatter the hazelnuts and orange segments over the fish, then pour brown butter overtop. Finish with fresh herbs and optional crispy parsley.

Variation: This dish is from One. At North 44 we instead make a classic brown butter with capers—about 1 tsp (5 mL) per fish. We also remove the roe sac, dust it with flour, and fry it until golden to serve with the fish along with a side dish such as sautéed chanterelles with sweet peas.

Suggested wine: Alsatian Pinot Gris

Miso-Glazed Black Cod

Miso-glazed fish is a traditional Japanese dish that Chef Nobu Matsuhisa popularized in the West courtesy of his many outposts (London, New York, etc.). Nobu used black cod, Chef Ming Tsai favoured Chilean sea bass—it works with any oily fish. Most recipes call for a higher ratio of miso to liquid than ours, and deploy the marinade as is. We prefer the flavour derived from using less miso and reducing the marinade, simmering away the alcohol in the process.
SERVES 4

1½ cups (375 mL) sake
1 cup (250 mL) aji-mirin (sweet Japanese rice wine)
¾ cup (175 mL) shiro-miso (white miso)
¼ cup (50 mL) granulated sugar
4 skinless Alaskan black cod fillets, about
    5 oz (150 g) each
2 tbsp (30 mL) vegetable oil

GARNISH
Chive oil (page 232)

POSSIBLE ACCOMPANIMENTS: Soubise rice cake (page 195), braised variegated chard (page 180), sautéed bok choi with Asian glaze (page 224)

Whisk together the sake, aji-mirin, shiro-miso, and sugar in a saucepan and simmer gently for an hour, until it coats the back of a spoon. Remove all but ½ cup (125 mL) or so and refrigerate until cool; set aside the remaining marinade at room temperature. Add fish fillets to the chilled marinade, turn them until they are completely coated, and then leave to rest at room temperature for 30 to 60 minutes.

Preheat oven to 425°F (220°C).

Heat an ovenproof nonstick skillet on medium-high, and heat the vegetable oil. Cautiously lower the fish fillets into the pan, standing as far back as possible to avoid the inevitable splatter. Discard the marinade. When the first side is caramelized, flip the fillets and immediately transfer the pan to the oven. Roast for 7 to 8 minutes—the fish will flake very easily once it is properly cooked.

Plate the fish and drizzle a little of the reserved room-temperature marinade around it—along with a little chive oil, if desired.

Tip: For all its virtues, black cod when raw is one of those fish whose pin bones are singularly resistant to removal. Tweezers will not work; the only way to create a true boneless cod fillet is to cut out the bones along with the flesh around them and in the process divide the fillet lengthwise. Your fishmonger will cut it for you this way—but only if you order it that way ahead of time.

Suggested wine: an aromatic Alsatian white or New World Pinot Noir

Crisp-Skinned Tasmanian Sea Trout with Charred-Tomato Risotto

The exquisite Tasmanian sea trout is a farmed steelhead trout raised in the enviably clean, brackish waters off the coast of Tasmania. Both its flesh and its skin are vibrantly coloured, the flavour hits all the bright notes of a fine Atlantic salmon, and its fat content makes it both easy to cook and a pleasure to eat. The acidity of the charred tomatoes in the risotto makes a perfect counterpoint to the fish's rich flesh. Adding the butter sauce is not strictly necessary, but you will find that the mix is sublime. SERVES 4

2 Roma tomatoes, halved, cored, and seeded
4 tbsp (60 mL) olive oil
Salt and black pepper
1 batch risotto (page 111)
4 Tasmanian sea trout fillets, about 6 oz (175 g) each, skin on
White pepper
½ cup (125 mL) frothed butter sauce (optional; page 229)

GARNISH
Sprigs of chervil, pea shoots, or the like

Preheat grill on high. Toss the tomato halves in 1 tbsp (15 mL) of the oil, season with salt and black pepper, and grill them until well charred on both sides. Chop the tomatoes.

Prepare risotto according to the directions on page 111, replacing the bacon, peas, and foie gras mousse with the charred tomato for flavouring.

Meanwhile, set a rack in the upper third of the oven and preheat oven to 375°F (190°C).

About halfway through cooking the risotto, place a large cast-iron or heavy-bottomed ovenproof nonstick skillet over medium heat. Pat the fish fillets dry and sprinkle the skin side with a little salt and white pepper. Scatter additional salt in the hot, dry skillet, and place the fillets in it skin side down. Sear for 2 or 3 minutes, sprinkle with salt and white pepper, and without turning the fish, transfer the pan to the oven. Cook until medium-rare—7 to 10 minutes, depending on thickness.

Begin plating with a portion of risotto. Perch a fillet on top of each serving crispy-skin side up. If you choose, pour frothed butter sauce all around. Garnish and serve.

Substitutions: Top-quality Atlantic salmon is a perfectly suitable stand-in for the sea trout. So is wild Arctic char. And when spring peas are in season they make for an excellent alternative to the tomatoes in the risotto.

Suggested wine: light Chianti

Butter-Poached Lobster with Sautéed Spinach and Shaved Truffle

Of the myriad ways to cook the lobster, none unfailingly delivers such a supple and decadent result as slow-poaching it in *beurre monté*. Here we present the luxurious dish with its own shell as a serving basket, wilted greens, and—why not?—truffle shavings. SERVES 2

2 live lobsters, about 2¼ lb (1.1 kg) each, par-cooked
    and shelled (page 237), tail shells and roe reserved
2 tbsp (30 mL) dry vermouth
1 lb (450 g) butter
1 batch wilted spinach or chard (page 180)
1 cup (250 mL) butter sauce (page 229)
Truffle shavings to taste

Turn the lobster tail shells into baskets as described on page 80. Prepare a *beurre monté* with the vermouth and butter as described on page 8.

Halve the tail meat lengthwise. Finish cooking the lobster tails and claws in the *beurre monté* for 4 or 5 minutes. Mound the wilted greens at the centre of two warmed plates. Place the lobster shell baskets on top of the greens. Retrieve the tail pieces from the *beurre monté* and place them back in their shells, but reversed, so that they sit perched on top of them. Place the claws on top of the tails. Froth the butter sauce—adding the reserved roe to the mix if you so choose. Drizzle the sauce all over the lobster and follow with truffle shavings.

Suggested wine: New World Chardonnay

Steamed Clams and Chorizo with Tomato Broth

The combination of steamed clams, chorizo, garlic, and chili-spiked tomato broth speaks loudly of the sun and a country far away with a coastline eminently more hospitable than our own. That said, this rustic Mediterranean meal for two in a bowl makes for a seductively transporting lunch in summer or winter just about anywhere. SERVES 2

1½ tbsp (23 mL) minced onion
1 tbsp (15 mL) olive oil
½ cup (125 mL) roughly chopped cured chorizo
¼ cup (50 mL) canned whole Roma tomatoes, crushed
2 tbsp (30 mL) Spanish sofrito (page 244)
1 tsp (5 mL) chopped oil-preserved red chili
3 lb (1.5 kg) clams, scrubbed
¼ cup (50 mL) white wine
1 cup (250 mL) fish stock (page 246)
1 tbsp (15 mL) whipped butter (page 251)
½ tsp (2 mL) lemon juice
2 tbsp (30 mL) chopped mixed parsley, oregano, and cilantro
1 whole scallion, sliced
Salt and pepper

SUGGESTED ACCOMPANIMENT: Crusty bread

In a large sauté pan, sweat the onions in olive oil over medium heat for about a minute, and then add the chorizo. When the sausage is heated through and its paprika-tinged fat is beginning to liquefy and escape, add the tomatoes, sofrito, and chili. Sauté a minute longer. Add the clams and immediately deglaze the pan with the wine. Once that has reduced by about a third, add the fish stock. Bring to a simmer and then cover the pot. When after 5 to 7 minutes the clams have popped open, stir the pot to check for any that have not done so and discard them. Now add the butter, lemon juice, half the chopped herbs, and half the scallion, and season lightly. Stir again. Taste and correct seasonings if necessary. Transfer the clams to a large, warm serving bowl, pour the sauce over top, and sprinkle with the remaining chopped herbs and scallion.

Suggested wine: crisp Sauvignon Blanc or light Rioja—or a cold lager

Bouillabaisse

In Marseilles, where bouillabaisse was born, they say that you cannot even pretend to make the soup without their local rascasse, or scorpionfish. But the fact of the matter is that you can make a delicious bouillabaisse with whatever fish or shellfish you please, so long as you start out with a fine fish stock and infuse it with saffron. SERVES 4

2 quarts (2 L) fish stock (page 246)
1 large pinch saffron threads
2 tbsp (30 mL) olive oil
½ medium carrot, julienned
½ yellow or 1 small white onion, julienned
¼ fennel bulb, julienned
½ leek, white part only, julienned
½ clove garlic, very thinly sliced
3 strips of orange peel, pith removed
1 small oil-preserved red chili, sliced
2 sprigs thyme
1 bay leaf
½ cup (125 mL) white wine
Salt and pepper

1 cup (250 mL) tomato concassé (page 249)
8 clams, scrubbed
1 skinless black cod fillet, about 6 oz (175 g),
　　cut into 4 pieces
8 mussels, bearded and scrubbed
8 medium shrimp, shelled and deveined
4 large sea scallops, halved crosswise
1 small lobster, about 1¼ lb (625g),
　　cooked and shelled (page 237)
1 tbsp (15 mL) whipped butter (page 251)
1 tbsp (15 mL) minced Italian parsley
8 slices of baguette, toasted
1 cup (250 mL) rouille (page 243)

Bring the fish stock to a simmer. Add the saffron, cover, turn off the heat, and allow to steep. Heat the oil in a large saucepan and begin to sauté the carrots and onions. As soon as they begin to soften—in 2 or 3 minutes—add the fennel, leek, garlic, orange peel, chili, thyme, and bay leaf. Do not allow the vegetables to colour—as soon as they begin to wilt, deglaze with the wine and then season. Strain the saffron-infused fish stock through a sieve into the saucepan. Bring to a simmer. Add the tomatoes, clams and cod, then cover the pot. Three or four minutes later, add the mussels, shrimp, and scallops; cover again. Two minutes later, follow with the cooked lobster. By the time the lobster is heated through, all the shellfish should have opened—discard any that haven't. Stir in the whipped butter and sprinkle with parsley. Ladle the soup into warm serving bowls and serve with the toast and a large ramekin of rouille.

Substitutions: The list of seafood included with this recipe is as much a guide to quantity as to selection. All shellfish fits well in a bouillabaisse: simply select whatever looks best at the fishmonger. Similarly, nearly all white fish will work: scorpionfish, Atlantic cod, monkfish, sea bass, and any number of others will taste just as good as or better in the mix than the black cod.

Suggested wine: white Rioja or Sicilian whites

Meat and Poultry

As I understand it—and I like to think that I understand it well—this is what people like to eat most. So we made it the largest section of the book. Of course the rich subjects of pork, beef, bison, venison, lamb, duck, rabbit, chicken, and squab cannot be thoroughly covered in seventeen recipes. But the dishes outlined here do go some long way to showcasing their potential.

I hope you take on these recipes in the spirit that was intended. And that was that whenever the recipes allow for it, you will enjoy them family-style, sharing them at the table in an appropriately casual, convivial way rather than plating them in the kitchen. The suggested side dishes are only that—suggestions. Pick something else from the book if you like. Or substitute your favourite sides. As long as you enjoy it, you are doing it right.

Slow-Braised Beef Brisket

A good half-century before lamb shanks, beef short ribs, and pork belly set out on this now familiar path, beef brisket set the trend for cheap cuts of meat that, when prepared right, tasted so good that they very soon stopped being cheap at all. But if the price of brisket is no longer low, the cut remains a relative bargain, especially when paired with this recipe, which is both simple and foolproof. SERVES 10

1 beef brisket, 8 to 10 lb (3.5 to 4.5 kg), trimmed
1½ cups (375 mL) dry rub (page 231)
4 Spanish onions, sliced ¼-in (5 mm) thick
Salt and pepper

POSSIBLE ACCOMPANIMENTS: Ramp or chive mashed potatoes (page 192), French fries (page 194), roasted Brussels sprouts (page 189)

Preheat oven to 325°F (160°C).

Dust the brisket with 1 cup (250 mL) of the dry rub, covering the meat completely. Scatter half the onions over the bottom of a roasting pan large enough to generously accommodate the brisket. Sprinkle the remaining dry rub over the onions. Add the brisket fat side up and top with the remaining onions. Add cold water to the pan until the brisket is two-thirds submerged. Heat on the stove until the water begins to steam slightly, then cover the pan tightly with heavy-duty foil and transfer to the oven.

After 2 hours, turn the brisket. Cover it once again with half the onions and then seal the foil tightly over the pan. Two hours later, check the brisket for tenderness by prodding it with a fork: if the meat feels springy and elastic rather than soft and pliant, flip the brisket once more, return it to the oven, and check it every 30 minutes until it is very tender.

When the beef is finally tender, remove it from the pan, cover with foil, and set it aside to rest. Skim or drain as much fat as possible from the roasting pan, and then, in batches if necessary, purée the onions with the braising liquid in a blender. Pass it through a fine-mesh sieve into a saucepan. Reheat and adjust seasonings. Slice the brisket—against the grain of the meat—to desired thickness. Serve drizzled generously with braised onion sauce, with extra sauce served on the side.

Tip: See page 88 for the ideal treatment for leftovers.

Suggested wine: New World Merlot or Châteauneuf-du-Pape

Beef Two Ways with *Jus Naturel* and Fresh Horseradish

Good cooking seldom involves reinventing the wheel but does always strive to improve upon it. Such is the thinking here as applied to the perennially familiar "meat and two veg"—wherein our flavour upgrade now delivers two meats and three vegetables to the benefit of each. The harmonious mix is then dressed with a sauce derived from a pure braising liquid that is rich in flavour but undisguised by red wine or brandy or any other typical but unnecessary enhancement. **SERVES 6**

1½ lb (750 g) short ribs, cut 3 in (7 cm) thick
4 tbsp (60 mL) olive oil
Salt and coarsely ground pepper
1 Spanish onion, chopped
1 celery stalk, chopped
6 cloves garlic, smashed
1 cup (250 mL) chopped carrots
1½ ripe Roma tomatoes, topped and quartered
1 cup (250 mL) white wine
4 cups (1 L) white chicken stock (page 246)

2 sprigs thyme
2 bay leaves
2 well-marbled dry-aged strip loin steaks,
    about 1 lb (450 g) each
1 tbsp (15 mL) olive oil
¼ cup (50 mL) veal jus (optional; page 247)
3 tbsp (45 mL) whipped butter (page 251)
Fine olive oil
6 pinches of fleur de sel
Freshly grated horseradish

POSSIBLE ACCOMPANIMENTS: A posh interpretation: fried truffled gnocchi (page 235), fava bean ragout (page 191), and sautéed spinach (page 180)

A rustic interpretation: chive mashed potatoes (page 192), roasted variegated beets (page 189), and braised Swiss chard (page 180)

Preheat oven to 325°F (160°C).

Rub short ribs lightly with some of the olive oil and season them generously with salt and pepper. Set an ovenproof pot large enough to accommodate the ribs in a single layer over medium-high heat, and heat 2 tbsp (30 mL) of the olive oil. Brown the ribs on all sides—approximately 10 minutes. Remove to a platter.

Pour off most of the fat. Heat the remaining 2 tbsp (30 mL) olive oil over medium-low, then add the onions and salt them lightly. Sweat the onions until translucent. Add the celery, garlic, and carrots; continue to sweat, stirring regularly—do not let the vegetables brown. Add the tomatoes. When the vegetables have softened, deglaze with the wine, and when that has reduced by half, return the short ribs to the pot. Add chicken stock to cover, bring to a simmer, add the herbs, cover the pot, and transfer to the oven.

Check the ribs after 1½ hours, turning them if they are not completely covered with stock. Expect a cooking time between 3 and 4 hours, but test for tenderness after 2½ hours—and every half-hour after that. The meat should be pulling away from the bone and will yield easily to being pierced with a fork.

Transfer the ribs to a much smaller pot. Set a sieve over the pot and strain in enough of the braising liquid to cover the ribs. Strain the remaining liquid into a separate pot, pressing hard on the vegetables with a wooden spoon to work some of them through the sieve. In a blender, purée the majority of the vegetables; set aside. Reduce the braising liquid until the intensity of its flavour is pleasing; set aside.

Thoroughly heat a grill or cast-iron skillet for the steaks. If using a skillet, scatter it with salt. Cook steaks to desired doneness. Allow them to rest for 10 minutes. Meanwhile, add veal jus to the reserved braising liquid—or thicken it with the puréed reserved vegetables, a little at a time until desired consistency is attained. Adjust seasonings. Reheat the short ribs in their braising liquid. Cut the steaks into ¼-inch (5 mm) slices. Whisk the butter into the thickened sauce and froth it with a hand wand.

Arrange gnocchi or mashed potatoes in the centre of six shallow bowls. To one side of that, place four or five slices of steak; to the other, place about a 3-oz (90 g) portion of short rib. Place chosen vegetable accompaniments in between. Pour the sauce all around. Follow with a drizzle of top-quality olive oil, a pinch of fleur de sel, and some freshly grated horseradish.

Suggested wine: aged Barolo or Napa Cabernet

Asian-Glazed Pork Belly

The pork belly has long starred on the plate via the smokehouse, as bacon, but over the last decade finally outgrew that long-time supporting role and enjoyed a moment in the sun as it took centre stage in all its fatty glory. This edition, wherein three days adrift in an aromatic brine are followed by braising, pressing, and finally a quick roast, is seductively flavoursome—in a word, addictive. SERVES 6

½ cup (125 mL) kosher salt
¼ cup (50 mL) granulated sugar
¼ cup (50 mL) honey
¼ cup (50 mL) smashed garlic cloves
1 tbsp (15 mL) coriander seeds
1 tbsp (15 mL) black peppercorns
6 bay leaves
2 kaffir lime leaves
¼ bunch thyme

¼ bunch cilantro
1 small knob ginger, thinly sliced
1 stalk lemongrass, smashed
4 star anise, broken
3 lb (1.5 kg) pork belly, in one piece, skin on
2 quarts (2 L) pork or white chicken stock (page 144)
¼ cup (50 mL) vegetable oil
1 cup (250 mL) Asian glaze (page 224)

SUGGESTED ACCOMPANIMENTS: Soubise rice cakes (page 195), wilted greens (page 180)

In a Dutch oven large enough to hold the pork snugly, combine the salt, sugar, honey, garlic, coriander seeds, peppercorns, bay leaves, lime leaves, thyme, cilantro, ginger, lemongrass, and star anise with 5 cups (1.25 L) cold water. Bring to a boil, then reduce heat and simmer, stirring, until the salt and sugar dissolve. Then chill. Once cooled, completely submerge the pork in the brine (add cold water if necessary to cover). Refrigerate for 3 days.

Preheat oven to 325°F (160°C).

Remove the pork from the brine (discarding the brine), rinse under cold running water, and pat dry. Bring the stock to a simmer. Place the pork in a roasting pan or casserole dish just large enough to accommodate the slab, cover with the stock, and transfer to the oven. Check the stock level periodically and top it up if evaporation leaves the pork exposed. After 2½ hours test the pork for tenderness. If it does not yet yield easily when prodded with a fork, braise for another 30 minutes—and carry on thus until the meat is very tender.

Remove the pork from the braising liquid (discarding the liquid) and transfer to a baking sheet to cool. Cover it with a sheet of parchment paper, then with a second baking sheet, add weight (bricks, tins of tomatoes, a small case of beer, what have you), and refrigerate overnight.

Preheat oven to 400°F (200°C).

Remove the skin from the pork and cut the pork into six equal portions. Heat the vegetable oil in a large skillet over medium-high heat until it is nearly smoking, then sear the pork on all sides until crisp and golden brown. Transfer to a baking dish, brush with the glaze, and transfer to the oven. After 10 minutes turn the pork and glaze the second side. Roast for another 5 to 10 minutes, until the glaze is tacky and the pork is thoroughly heated through.

Suggested wine: spicy Zinfandel or rich Viognier

Roast Rack of Pork with Maple-Whisky Glaze and Sautéed Peaches

Traditionally, pork was butchered in the fall, which—aside from fat content—goes some way to explaining why it so enjoys the company of braised fall fruits like peaches and apples. The loin is one of its best cuts, and when cooked whole as a rack it yields a texture eminently more satisfying than when it has been divided up into its constituent chops. The maple-whisky glaze ably completes the flavour trifecta—unless your butcher can provide the skin for crackling, which is even better. SERVES 4

1 4-rib rack of pork, about 3 lb (1.5 kg)
2 tbsp (30 mL) basic marinade (page 225)
Salt and pepper
3 tbsp (45 mL) olive oil
½ cup (125 mL) maple-whisky glaze (page 237)
1 batch sautéed peaches (page 227)

SUGGESTED ACCOMPANIMENTS: Chive or roasted garlic mashed potatoes (page 192), wilted greens (page 180)

Preheat oven to 350°F (180°C).

Massage the pork with the marinade and season it generously. Heat the oil in a skillet on medium-high, and sear the pork on all sides until nicely browned. Place the pork bone side down on a rack in a roasting rack and transfer to the oven. Roast for about 90 minutes—or until the internal temperature reaches 140°F (60°C). About 5 minutes before it is ready, brush the pork all over with maple-whisky glaze. Transfer pork to a serving platter and let rest for 15 to 20 minutes while you prepare the peaches.

Surround the pork with peaches cut side up. Drain fat from the roasting pan and drizzle the remaining pan juices over the peaches, pooling it in their cavities. Carve at the table.

Substitutions: A small 4-rib rack of whey-fed pork makes an ideal roast for two. This type of pork is usually sold with its skin on. If you choose that option or manage to procure a full-sized rack with its skin attached, omit the maple glaze and instead serve the pork with its crackling and herb tapenade (page 235). Use a very sharp knife to score the skin well before roasting. Then rub the skin thoroughly with salt, pushing it into the incisions. Do not rub the skin with basic marinade or oil, and sear only the exposed flesh. If the skin nonetheless fails to get crispy before the meat is done, baste it with sizzling-hot oil while the rack rests. Lastly, if peaches are unavailable, serve the pork with Riesling-braised apples (page 227) or apple sauce (page 227).

Tip: Ask your butcher not to trim the rack too much, as external fat helps to keep it moist while roasting. If the rack still appears lean, ask your butcher to bard it.

Suggested wine: rich Viognier or Australian GSM

Hong Kong Style Pork Ribs

The braising liquid for these pork ribs provides a perfect balance of heat, tang, and sweetness. And most of the work can be done ahead of time, leaving you to merely finish the ribs on the grill once your guests arrive. **SERVES 6 AS AN APPETIZER OR 4 AS A MAIN COURSE**

4 racks pork side ribs, about 1½ lb (750 g) each
2 cans (16 oz/650 mL) Sapporo
½ cup (125 mL) light Japanese soy sauce
½ cup (125 mL) maple syrup
½ cup (125 mL) rice wine vinegar
½ cup (125 mL) barbecue sauce (page 225)
2 bay leaves
1 tbsp (15 mL) cracked black pepper
1 tbsp (15 mL) chopped garlic

1 tbsp (15 mL) sambal oelek
½ lemon, sliced
Salt and pepper

GARNISH
2 tbsp (30 mL) minced chives
1 cup (250 mL) crème fraîche
¼ cup (50 mL) Dijon mustard
Lemon juice to taste

SUGGESTED ACCOMPANIMENTS: French fries (page 194) or aromatic rice and wilted greens (page 180). Beef ribs are better suited to herb tapenade (page 235) than crème fraîche.

Preheat oven to 375°F (190°C).

Arrange the ribs meaty side down in a roasting pan, preferably in a single layer. Combine all other ingredients in a bowl, stir well, and pour over the ribs. Cover the pan tightly with foil and transfer to the oven. After 45 minutes carefully remove foil, turn the ribs, and reseal. After an hour check the ribs for doneness: the meat should be just beginning to pull away from the bone.

Transfer the ribs to a clean roasting pan. Strain the braising liquid into a large measuring cup. Pour enough liquid over the ribs to submerge them completely. (Although the ribs can be finished immediately, their flavour will be better if you set them aside, covered in braising liquid, in the refrigerator overnight or up to several days.) Let the remaining braising liquid sit until the fat separates completely, then skim or pour it off. Transfer the liquid to a saucepan and reduce by about half—until it coats the back of a spoon.

Preheat grill on its lowest setting; brush rack with oil. Remove the ribs from the braising liquid (discarding the liquid) and transfer them to the grill meat side down. Brush them with the reduced braising liquid, turn, and brush again. Continue turning and glazing, watching that the sugar in the sauce does not burn, until the ribs are heated through and nicely coloured.

Cut the ribs, arrange on a large platter, drizzle with extra sauce, season with salt and pepper, sprinkle with chives, and serve with ramekins of crème fraîche combined with mustard and a few drops of lemon juice.

Substitutions: This same recipe can be used for pork back ribs, beef ribs, and even beef short ribs—but each will require a longer braising time than the side ribs. Test for doneness the same way. Heat larger ribs gently in their braising liquid before placing them on the grill.

Tip: When cutting a rack of ribs, run your knife as closely as possible along one of the two bones that you're cutting between, and then continue favouring that side all the way along the rack. That way, each rib will have a lot of meat on one side and almost nothing on the other, which makes them easier and more enjoyable to eat.

Suggested wine: Zinfandel or Viognier

Slow-Roasted Pork Shoulder with Gravy

Most restaurant cooking happens fast—very fast—because there is no other way to serve several hundred people a multi-course lunch in under two hours. But precisely because of that mad rush, slow-cooked meats that can be finished and plated *à la minute* have considerable appeal for efficiency of service. This superb slow-roasted pork shoulder from Bymark is a perennial dinnertime favourite there—and again the next day, reconfigured as an open-faced sandwich in a Yorkshire pudding (see page 89). **SERVES 10 TO 12**

1 boneless pork shoulder, 6 to 7 lb (about 3 kg), tied

BRINE
½ large carrot, diced
1 celery stalk, diced
1 medium Spanish onion, diced
1 nub ginger, sliced
5 cloves garlic, smashed
2 Thai chilies, split and seeded
1 bay leaf
1 tbsp (15 mL) mustard seeds
½ tbsp (7 mL) coriander seeds

2 whole cloves
1 star anise
1 cup (250 mL) granulated sugar
½ cup (125 mL) kosher salt

GRAVY
2 tbsp (30 mL) flour
2 cups (500 mL) white chicken stock (page 246), hot
1 tbsp (15 mL) gastrique (page 234)
Pinch each of salt and pepper
2 tbsp (30 mL) whipped butter (page 251)

SUGGESTED ACCOMPANIMENTS: Yorkshire pudding (page 89), herb tapenade (page 235), Riesling-braised apples (page 227) or spiced apples (page 159), chive or garlic mashed potatoes (page 192), roasted Brussels sprouts (page 189) or roasted root vegetables (page 184)

In a large pot combine all ingredients for the brine. Add 3 quarts (3 L) cold water, bring to a boil, then reduce heat and simmer until the vegetables are soft—about 30 minutes. Refrigerate until cool. Add the pork to the brine, adding more water to cover if necessary. Marinate the pork for 24 hours. Transfer the pork to a rack set in a roasting pan and return it to refrigerator, uncovered, for another 24 hours. Discard brine.

Preheat oven to 325°F (160°C).

Roast the pork for 4 to 5 hours—until the skin is crisp and the meat comes apart when prodded with a fork. Let the pork rest while you finish the side dishes and make the gravy.

Pour off fat from the pan juices and reserve (for Yorkshire pudding). Over high heat, reduce the pan juices by half. Lower heat to medium-low, add the flour, and stir to thicken for 3 to 4 minutes. Whisk 3 oz (90 mL) of the chicken stock at a time into the roux until all the stock is incorporated. Strain the gravy through a fine-mesh sieve into a clean saucepan on low heat. Adjust the acidity by adding a few drops of the gastrique at a time. Correct seasonings. Remove from heat, whisk in the butter, and transfer to a gravy boat.

Suggested wine: Australian GSM blends, Vouvray, or Chenin Blanc

Spring Lamb Stew with Mint-Infused Sweet Pea Ravioli

Braised meats are often thought of as the cornerstone of heavy autumnal meals. Yet this light lamb stew instead speaks softly but most assertively of springtime. The version with the ravioli and freshly prepared vegetables is a restaurant-style take appropriate for weekend entertaining at home. But we have also included a much-simplified cottage edition. Neither is better; it simply comes down to where you are, how much time you have, and what sort of mood you are in. SERVES 4

1 medium Spanish onion
1 leek, some green included, washed
4 celery stalks
1 medium carrot, peeled
2 lb (1 kg) boneless lamb shoulder
2 tbsp (30 mL) basic marinade (page 225)
Salt and cracked black pepper
3 tbsp (45 mL) olive oil
3 cloves garlic, smashed
4 bay leaves
1 cup (250 mL) white wine
6 cups (1.5 L) white chicken stock (page 246)
3 tbsp (45 mL) whipped butter (page 251)

RAVIOLI
2 cups (500 mL) sweet peas, blanched
¼ cup (50 mL) grated Parmigiano-Reggiano

¼ cup (50 mL) lemon juice
8 mint leaves, cut into chiffonade
2 tbsp (30 mL) olive oil
Salt and pepper
1 batch pasta dough (page 239)
1 egg, lightly beaten

VEGETABLES
2 cups (500 mL) some combination of sweet peas,
    young carrots, young parsnips, and pearl onions,
    blanched and shocked in ice water
1 tbsp (15 mL) olive oil
1 tbsp (15 mL) white wine
Salt and pepper

GARNISH
Mint chiffonade or minced parsley

Preheat oven to 350°F (180°C)

For the refined version, coarsely chop the onion, leek, celery, and carrot; for the rustic take, cut them into 1-inch (2.5 cm) pieces. Massage the lamb all over with the marinade and season it generously. Heat the oil in a Dutch oven on medium-high, then sear the lamb well—about 5 or 6 minutes per side. Remove the lamb, then lower the heat to medium-low. Add the vegetables, garlic, and bay leaves. Season the vegetables and cook, stirring now and then, until they begin to caramelize. Return the lamb to the pot, raise the heat, and deglaze with the wine. When that has almost completely evaporated, add enough stock to cover, bring to a simmer, adjust seasonings, cover the pot and transfer it to the oven. Cook for 90 minutes, then check lamb for fork-tenderness. Keep cooking for another 30 to 45 minutes if necessary.

continued

For the rustic edition, prepare mashed potatoes (page 192). For the refined version, make ravioli: Whiz the peas, Parmesan, lemon juice, mint, olive oil, and seasonings together in a food processor. Roll out pasta dough and make 15 ravioli according to the directions on page 98.

Remove the lamb from the pot and break it into pieces. For the cottage edition, skim the fat from the pot, return the lamb, and serve with its braising vegetables, mashed potatoes, and a sprinkle of mint chiffonade.

For the refined version, put the lamb pieces in a bowl with some braising liquid, cover, and keep warm. Discard the bay leaves and then whiz the braising liquid in a blender. Strain the sauce into a large measuring cup and allow it to settle. Skim the fat, and then transfer the sauce to a clean pot. Reheat and adjust seasonings.

Lightly oil the tray of a steamer, place the ravioli inside, dab with a little butter, and steam for 2 minutes or until the pasta is cooked. Meanwhile, quickly sauté the blanched vegetables in the olive oil and then deglaze with the wine and season. Add whipped butter to the lamb sauce and froth with a hand wand. Portion out lamb onto warm plates, scatter vegetables overtop, and top each portion with 3 ravioli. Pour the sauce over the ravioli and garnish lightly.

Suggested wine: McLaren Vale or Washington State Cabernet

Venison Stew

Venison is an ideal braising meat, for it is lean but inclined to tenderness, and assertively flavoursome without ever being excessively gamy. This hearty stew is perfect for a winter night. The array of colourful vegetables are separately cooked so that each one preserves its colour, texture, and flavour. SERVES 6

2 lb (1 kg) venison stewing meat, cut in
    1½-in (3 cm) cubes
Salt and cracked black pepper
½ cup (125 mL) vegetable oil
½ Spanish onion, diced
¼ cup (50 mL) flour
¼ cup (50 mL) red wine
2 bay leaves
1 clove garlic, thinly sliced
1 quart (1 L) veal stock (page 246)

1 medium beet, about ¼ lb (125 g), roasted and cubed
1 medium turnip, about ¼ lb (125 g), roasted and cubed
2 medium carrots, about ¼ lb (125 g), roasted and
    thickly sliced
½ bag pearl onions, about ¼ lb (125 g), blanched
    and roasted
¼ cup (50 mL) chopped parsley
1 tbsp (15 mL) minced thyme
1 tsp (5 mL) minced rosemary

SUGGESTED ACCOMPANIMENT: Chive mashed potatoes (page 192)

Preheat oven to 350°F (180°C).

Season the venison generously. Heat half the oil in a heavy-bottomed Dutch oven on medium-high. Sear the venison on all sides, and remove to a warm platter. Drain the fat from the pot, wipe it well with a cluster of paper towels, and place on medium heat. Add the remaining oil and cook the onions until translucent. Return the meat to the pot. Sift the flour over the meat and cook, stirring constantly to prevent sticking, for 3 minutes. Deglaze the pot with the wine. Add the bay leaves, garlic, and stock, bring to a simmer, cover, and transfer to the oven.

After 1 hour and 15 minutes, test the meat for tenderness: it should offer little resistance to the advancing fork. If it is not yet done, return the pot to the oven and test every 10 minutes. When the meat is done, add all the vegetables to the pot, along with the parsley, thyme, and rosemary. Stir, and simmer very briefly on the stovetop to heat through. Taste, and correct seasonings. Discard the bay leaf if you choose.

Substitutions: You may use beef or even chicken stock instead of veal stock to no deleterious effect, for the flavour of venison is so assertive that it will take over in the end all the same.

Shortcut: The vegetables included in the stew retain better texture and assert their flavour more distinctly if prepared separately and added at the very end as described, but you can of course cook them all together if you prefer and add them to the pot after its first 30 minutes in the oven. But note that red beets will colour the entire stew, so use white or yellow ones or none at all.

Suggested wine: Northern Rhône Syrah or cool-climate Australian Shiraz

Braised Venison Shank

This robust variation on the traditional Milanese osso buco applies some Canadian content to an Italian classic. It is a substantial dish, more appropriate to our winter than theirs, and perfect for serving on a cold winter's night. SERVES 6

3 bay leaves
2 sprigs thyme
2 sprigs rosemary
3 parsley stems
6 slices of venison shank, each 1½ in (4 cm)
   thick and about 10 oz (285 g)
¼ cup (50 mL) olive oil
Salt and cracked black pepper
1 medium onion, chopped

2 celery stalks, chopped
1 medium carrot, chopped
4 cloves garlic, chopped
2 Roma tomatoes, topped and quartered
2 cups (500 mL) red wine
4 quarts (4 L) beef or veal stock (page 246), hot

GARNISH
2 tbsp (30 mL) minced parsley or other mild greens

SUGGESTED ACCOMPANIMENTS: Chive mashed potatoes (page 192), roasted Brussels sprouts (page 189), roasted beets (page 189), Riesling-braised apples (page 227)

Preheat oven to 350°F (180°C).

Tie the bay leaves, thyme, rosemary, and parsley together into a bouquet garni. Tie a string snugly around each shank so that they will hold their shape as they cook. Massage them lightly with a little of the olive oil and season generously with salt and pepper. Heat 2 tbsp (30 mL) of the oil in a heavy-bottomed Dutch oven large enough to accommodate all the shanks in a single layer, then sear the shanks well on all sides. Remove and set aside. Pour off the scalded oil and replace with the remaining oil. Lower the heat to medium and add the onion, celery, carrot, and garlic. Sweat until they begin to wilt, then stir in the tomatoes. After a few minutes return the shanks to the pot along with the bouquet garni, then raise the heat and deglaze with the wine. When that has nearly evaporated, add enough stock to cover the shanks, and continue cooking until it has evaporated by half. Add stock to cover the shanks once more, bring to a simmer, cover the pot, and transfer to the oven. Turn the shanks carefully after 45 minutes. Cook until the meat is tender and pulling away from the bone—about 1 hour 45 minutes.

Transfer the shanks to a warm plate. Discard the bouquet garni and skim fat from the braising liquid. Purée in a blender and strain through a fine sieve. Reduce slightly if necessary, adjust seasonings, and return the shanks to the pot. Serve from the cooking pot or a large warm platter, the shanks well lubricated with sauce and sprinkled with parsley.

Suggested wine: Barossa Shiraz

Five-Spice Bison Tenderloin with Spiced Apple

Bison is a lean beast, and so, just as with beef—but even more so—its tenderloin must be cooked rare or it will be tender no more. When cooked properly, the meat will be succulent, its flavour beautifully complemented by the definitive Chinese spice mix known as five-spice. We echo some of its notes in the spicing for the accompanying braised apple, that most reliable of fruity counterpoints for game meats. **SERVES 6**

1 whole bison tenderloin, about 2 lb (1 kg),
    trimmed and tied
3 tbsp (45 mL) olive oil
1 tsp (5 mL) five-spice powder
Salt
Frothed butter sauce (optional; page 229)

SPICED APPLES
2 tsp (10 mL) olive oil
2 braising apples (preferably Fuji),
    peeled and cut into ¼-in (5 mm) dice
1 star anise
3 whole cloves
½ stick cinnamon
Pinch of salt
2 tbsp (30 mL) brown sugar
¼ cup (50 mL) Riesling

SUGGESTED ACCOMPANIMENTS: Risotto with sweet peas (page 113) or chive mashed potatoes (page 192), roasted sugar beets (page 189) enhanced with a few drops of chili oil (page 232), braised spinach or chard (page 180)

Preheat oven to 250°F (120°C).

Let bison rest at room temperature for 30 minutes, then pat dry with paper towels. Rub lightly with 2 tsp (10 mL) of the olive oil, sprinkle on all sides with five-spice powder, and season generously with salt. Heat a large, thick-bottomed nonstick skillet on medium-high. Heat the remaining oil, and then sear the bison on all sides until nicely browned—7 to 8 minutes. Transfer the bison to a rack in a shallow roasting dish and roast about 50 minutes—until a meat thermometer reads 115°F (46°C). Turn off oven and return the bison to the oven to rest for 10 to 15 minutes with the door ajar. The internal temperature should reach 125°F (50°C). Transfer bison to a carving board, tent with foil, and let rest another 10 minutes.

SPICED APPLES: Meanwhile, heat a small saucepan on medium-high and add the oil, apple, star anise, cloves, cinnamon, and a pinch of salt. Stir frequently to avoid excessive browning. As soon as the apples begin to take on colour, add the sugar and half the Riesling. Reduce to a thick syrup and repeat. Remove from the heat.

Carve the bison. Place a mound of risotto or mashed potato on each plate. Add two slices of bison, the selected vegetables. If desired, drizzle with butter sauce. Top the bison with a generous spoonful of spiced apple and serve.

Suggested wine: Merlot, Australian Shiraz

Rabbit with Grainy Mustard Sauce

Rabbit is a lovely, delicate meat, unjustly overlooked—likely because its leanness makes it easy to overcook to a state of dryness. But if you pay attention, there is little risk of that. And there is probably no other sauce that complements a properly braised rabbit as nicely as does the classic *sauce moutarde*. Ours forgoes the conventional cream and instead takes its body from stock and mustard alone. SERVES 6

2 rabbits, about 3½ lb (1.6 kg) each,
    trimmed and cut into 8 pieces (page 162)
Salt and white pepper
2 tbsp (30 mL) vegetable oil
1 medium Spanish onion, chopped
1 medium carrot, chopped
1 medium parsnip, chopped

1 celery stalk, chopped
6 cloves garlic, smashed
1 cup (250 mL) white wine
2 quarts (2 L) white chicken stock (page 246), hot
2 bay leaves
1 to 2 tbsp (15 to 30 mL) moutarde de Meaux
1 to 2 tbsp (15 to 30 mL) Dijon mustard

POSSIBLE ACCOMPANIMENTS: Halved boiled or steamed fingerling potatoes or chive mashed potatoes (page 192), or pappardelle lightly dressed with butter and parsley, along with roasted root vegetables such as carrots, parsnips, or beets (page 184)

Preheat oven to 350°F (180°C).

Season the rabbit generously. Heat the vegetable oil over medium-high heat in a heavy-bottomed 8-quart (8 L) ovenproof pot. Brown the rabbit pieces on all sides, in batches if necessary. Remove rabbit to a warm plate, lower heat to medium, and add the onion along with some salt. Cook for 5 minutes, stirring frequently to prevent the onions from browning. Add the carrot, parsnip, celery, and garlic. Cook only until wilted—do not brown. Deglaze quickly with the wine, then swiftly return rabbit to the pot along with any juices, placing the large hind legs at the bottom of the heap and the saddle and forelegs at the top.

Add 1 cup (250 mL) of the hot chicken stock to the pot—or enough to just cover the rabbit—and simmer, uncovered, for 5 minutes or until the liquid is reduced by about a third. Then add another cup and reduce. Continue adding and reducing stock—seasoning lightly as you go—leaving the rabbit just covered. Then add the bay leaves, cover the pot, and transfer to the oven. Braise about 40 minutes—until the meat starts to retreat from the bone and feels tender when pierced with a fork.

Transfer the rabbit pieces to a clean pot. Strain the braising liquid and splash a little over the rabbit to keep it moist; cover and set aside. Discard the bay leaves. Transfer the braised vegetables to a blender and blitz until smooth. Pass through a strainer into a clean pot, add the reserved braising liquid, and bring the mixture to a simmer. Stir in 1 tbsp (15 mL) of each mustard and adjust seasonings. Reduce until the sauce thickens; taste and add more mustard if necessary. Pour the sauce over the rabbit, heat through, and serve.

Tip: The reason you do not brown your vegetables is that the ideal mustard sauce for rabbit is light in colour and creamily silken in texture—never dark, strong, or sharp in flavour.

Suggested wine: a Cru Chablis or a young red Burgundy (preferably Beaune)

Rabbit Cassoulet

This version forgoes the traditional mutton, pork, goose, and duck in favour of a lean rabbit. The results are just as savoury. SERVES 4

1 rabbit, about 3½ lb (1.6 kg)
4 oz (125 g) pork back fat
7 cloves roasted garlic, squeezed (page 243)
1 tsp (5 mL) dried thyme
1 tsp (5 mL) dried juniper berries, ground
1 tsp (5 mL) yellow mustard seeds, ground
1 tsp (5 mL) salt
1 tsp (5 mL) pepper
3 feet (1 m) medium-width sausage casing
1½ cups (375 mL) dried navy or cannellini beans
2 whole cloves
1 yellow onion, peeled
1 quart (1 L) white chicken stock (page 246)

½ cup (125 mL) olive oil
Salt and pepper
2 quarts (2 L) duck fat
4 very thin slices of prosciutto
1 tbsp (15 mL) butter
1½ cups (375 mL) rabbit jus (page 249)
1 batch braised cipollini onions (page 197)
Tomato concassé (page 249), made with 6 Roma tomatoes
2 bunches collard greens, trimmed, blanched, and very coarsely chopped
1 bunch scallions, thinly sliced diagonally
3 tbsp (45 mL) whipped butter (page 251)
2 Riesling-braised quince (page 227)

PREPARE THE RABBIT: Cut off the hind legs and remove the thigh bones. Cut off the forelegs. Working carefully to keep them intact, cut away the long loins from the back. Separate all other meat from the bone, reserving meat and bones (for making the rabbit jus) separately. Set aside legs and loins in the refrigerator. Pass all other rabbit meat and the pork fat through a meat grinder equipped with a medium blade. Combine in a bowl with the garlic, thyme, juniper, mustard, salt and pepper, and mix well. Remove a small sample, sear it, taste, and adjust seasonings. Use a sausage funnel to feed the rabbit filling into the sausage casing. Tie off sausages at 6-inch (15 cm) lengths and set them aside in the refrigerator for at least 24 hours.

Meanwhile, rinse the beans and soak them for 24 hours.

Push whole cloves into the onion, place it in a pot with the drained beans, and add chicken stock to cover. Bring to a boil, lower heat, and simmer until the beans are tender—anywhere from 1½ to 2½ hours.

Meanwhile, preheat oven to 225°F (110°C). Season the rabbit legs (fore and hind) generously. Heat 3 tbsp (45 L) of the oil in a skillet and sear the outer sides of the legs until bronzed. Heat duck fat in an ovenproof saucepan to 200°F (95°C). Add the rabbit legs and transfer to the oven. Cook until tender—45 minutes for forelegs and 90 minutes for hind legs.

Increase heat to 400°F (200°C). Sear the sausages on all sides in 2 tbsp (30 mL) of the olive oil. Place the rabbit legs seared side down in an ovenproof skillet lined with parchment paper and transfer to the oven until heated through and well bronzed—10 to 15 minutes. Lightly season the rabbit loins and then spiral-wrap them in prosciutto. Sear in 1 tbsp (15 mL) oil and the butter for 45 to 60 seconds per side, then set aside to rest. Reheat the beans with the rabbit jus, and fold in the onions, tomato concassé, collard greens, and scallions. Taste, adjust seasonings, and fold in the whipped butter.

Pour the beans in the centre of a large serving plate. Slice the sausage and loins into 1-inch (2.5 cm) lengths and distribute over the beans. Place legs seared side up in the middle. Scatter the Riesling-braised quince overtop.

Suggested wine: Chablis, elegant Zinfandel, or Pinot Noir

Squab Two Ways with Chanterelle-Filled Cabbage Roll and Cauliflower Purée

Squab is one of the great roasting fowl, but the deep flavour, succulence, and exceptional texture of its breast will be completely ruined if it is cooked beyond the ruddy pink state of medium-rare—so don't. These birds are generally at their best in the autumn, and so we paired them with another pleasure of the season, chanterelles. SERVES 4

4 squab, about 1¼ lb (625 g) each
4 tbsp (60 mL) olive oil
Salt
2 slices lemon, about ¼ in (5 mm) thick, charred on grill or in dry skillet, halved
8 sage leaves
4 cloves garlic, smashed
1 tbsp (15 mL) five-spice powder
½ tsp (2 mL) white pepper
3 cups (750 mL) rendered duck fat
1 batch mushroom cabbage rolls (page 179), made with 8 oz (250 g) chanterelles
1 cup (250 mL) veal jus (page 247), hot
1 tbsp (15 mL) whipped butter (page 251)

CAULIFLOWER PURÉE
10 oz (300 g) cauliflower, thinly sliced
2½ cups (625 mL) milk
Pinch each of salt and white pepper
Tiny pinch of nutmeg

GARNISH
Sprigs of greens herbs, young greens, or 8 crispy sage leaves (page 180)

The day before cooking the squab, cut off the birds' heads at the base of the neck. Remove the top two joints of their wings along with the feet and reserve for stock. Trim off and discard any extra skin or fat. Pat the birds dry with paper towels, place them breast side up on a roasting rack, and allow to dry overnight uncovered in the refrigerator.

Preheat oven to 200°F (100°C).

continued

Cut the legs from each bird at the base of the thigh, cutting very carefully so as not to remove too much skin from the breast. Rub a few drops of olive oil over each bird. Insert a pinch of salt, the lemon, sage, and garlic into each cavity. Tie a string snugly around the bird lengthwise in a loop running under the neck, over the wings and around the cavity opening. Salt the exterior, pressing the crystals into the flesh. Season each bird generously with five-spice powder and a pinch of white pepper. Repeat for the legs, oiling and seasoning both sides.

Heat the duck fat in a small saucepan to 200°F (100°C). In a large ovenproof nonstick skillet on medium, heat the remaining olive oil. Brown the birds on all sides—about 10 minutes. Also sear the legs—but only on the fatty skin side. Set the birds aside on their roasting rack with the wing joins pointing in the same direction; set aside. Add the legs to the duck fat and transfer to the oven for 30 minutes, by which time the meat should be beginning to pull away from the bone. Transfer the legs to a small baking sheet and set aside. Increase oven to 425°F (220°C).

Meanwhile, make the cauliflower purée: Combine the cauliflower, milk, and seasonings in a small saucepan and cook according to the directions for cauliflower bisque on page 27, but add only a little reserved milk to the purée—the desired texture is thick but not excessively stiff. Keep warm.

Roast the squab, with wing joints near the back wall of the oven, until medium-rare—10 to 12 minutes. Remove from the oven (don't turn it off) and let rest in the roasting pan for 5 minutes.

Meanwhile, moisten the cabbage rolls with chicken stock and gently reheat them for 10 minutes in a 350°F (180°C) oven—or in the hot roasting oven for no more than 5 minutes, but be vigilant. Place the legs high in the oven to brown and crisp. Return the squab to the oven to crisp for 2 or 3 minutes.

Carefully fillet the breast halves from each squab. Add whipped butter to the veal jus and froth. Place a cabbage roll to one side of each plate along with a dollop of cauliflower purée. Prop up one breast half against the cabbage roll, follow with another, then the two legs. Spoon frothed sauce alongside. Garnish and serve.

Suggested wine: New World Pinot Noir, aged Burgundy, or an elegant Zinfandel

Duck Shepherd's Pie

Shepherds do not keep ducks—they keep sheep—which is why a proper shepherd's pie is made with leftover lamb or mutton, and never beef, as everyone seems to think (that's cottage pie). What with all the confusion, it seemed fair to play with the recipe again, and upgrade it not just with a filling made from exquisite duck confit but also with a luxurious infusion of truffle to enhance its potato topping. SERVES 4

4 confit duck legs (page 231), about 5 oz (150 g) each
3 medium carrots, cut in large dice
1 medium parsnip, cut in large dice
2 tbsp (30 mL) olive oil
1 cup (250 mL) braised cipollini or pearl onions
   (page 197)

1 cup (250 mL) cooked corn kernels
1 cup (250 mL) duck jus (page 249)
1 tbsp (15 mL) combined minced parsley and thyme
Salt and pepper
¼ cup (50 mL) truffle paste (optional)
1 batch basic mashed potatoes (page 192)

Preheat oven to 425°F (220°C).

Warm the confit. Carefully remove the skin from the legs. Shred the meat from the bones and set aside. Arrange the skins in a single layer in a skillet over low heat. Gently render the skins crisp, flipping them periodically. Meanwhile, sauté the carrots and parsnip in the oil over medium-high heat. When they have begun to soften and take on some colour, add the onions, corn, and duck meat. Stir, and then add the duck jus. Follow with half the fresh herbs and some salt and pepper. Stir, taste, and correct the seasonings. Transfer the duck mixture to four small (or one large) baking dishes.

Add the remaining herbs and the truffle paste, if using, to the mashed potatoes. Combine well, taste, and season. Cover the duck filling with a layer of the potatoes—either forkful by forkful or by piping them through a pastry bag. Bake until the topping is brown—15 to 20 minutes. Let rest briefly. Drain the crispy duck skins briefly on paper towels and then cut them into bite-size pieces. Arrange them in a pattern on top of the pie, standing upright in the mashed potatoes.

Substitutions: Some ducks (notably the foie gras–producing Moulard) are considerably larger than the delicate Pekin ducks that we use to make confit at the restaurants. If your confit weighs in nearer to 7 oz (200 g), simply use three legs instead of four. Secondly, while the duck jus lends this dish a wonderful richness, not having the time to make some is not reason in itself to abandon the dish. For a shortcut, after adding the duck to the vegetables, deglaze the pan with 1 to 2 tbsp (15 to 30 mL) red wine; once that has completely reduced, sift 1 to 2 tsp (5 to 10 mL) of flour over the mixture. Stir well for 2 to 3 minutes, then add 1 cup (250 mL) white or dark chicken stock and simmer until it thickens.

Suggested wine: Malbec or an earthy Pinot Noir

Duck Three Ways with Soubise Rice Cakes and Seasonal Berries

No other meat or fowl lends itself to a trio of starkly different but complementary preparations quite so amenably and exquisitely as the duckling. Perhaps the bird enjoys an unfair advantage in that it packs the finest offal on earth: foie gras. In any case, the following combination of *cuisse en confit*, seared magret, and foie gras dressed with its own jus cut with fresh berries will please anyone of refined appetite. SERVES 4

1 duck magret, about 12 oz (375 g)	Salt and pepper
1 tbsp (15 mL) olive oil	4 soubise rice cakes (page 195), shaped but not cooked
Pinch each of ground juniper and white pepper	1 cup (250 mL) duck jus (page 249)
2 sprigs thyme	¼ cup (50 mL) berries (elderberries, currants,
1 sprig sage	blueberries, pickled blueberries, etc.)
2 confit duck legs (page 231), about 5 oz (150 g) each	4 slices fresh foie gras, about 3 oz (90 g) each, deveined

Use a very sharp knife to score the skin and fat of the magret very nearly down to the flesh itself—or, if you prefer a leaner magret, trim off the skin altogether, leaving behind only a uniformly thin layer of fat, about ⅛ inch (3 mm), and score that lightly instead. Rub the breast on all sides with a little of the olive oil, sprinkle with the juniper and pepper, and adorn each side with thyme and sage. Wrap in plastic wrap and refrigerate overnight.

Preheat oven to 425°F (220°C).

Heat a skillet with the remaining olive oil over medium-low heat. Remove the sprigs of herbs from the duck breast, salt both sides generously, and add it to the pan skin side down. While the fat is rendering from the magret (this will take longer if the skin was left on), place the two legs of confit skin side down on parchment paper in an ovenproof skillet. Roast until crisp—about 15 minutes. Meanwhile, when you can see that the heat has penetrated beyond the fat of the magret and started to cook the breast itself, flip it and cook the second side for 4 minutes. Do not cook beyond medium-rare. When the magret is done to your liking, set it aside to rest, keeping warm.

Fry the rice cakes. Meanwhile, warm the duck jus in a small saucepan and add the berries. Heat a heavy skillet on medium-high, and when it is piping hot, score the foie gras slices on one side, salt them, and add to the pan scored side down. Sear for about a minute, flip, and sear the second side for 45 seconds or so (depending on thickness). Slice the magret about ¼ inch (5 mm) thick. Place a rice cake at the centre of each warm plate, and around it fan some slices of magret, ½ leg of duck confit cut from the bone, and the seared foie gras. Drizzle the sauce and berries all around.

Suggested wine: New World Pinot Noir, Cru Riesling, or Alsatian Pinot Gris

Roast Suprêmes of Chicken with Mushroom-Stuffed Thighs

Chicken is the most versatile of fowl. Since we offer it up once in these pages in its most rustic form, we thought we should illustrate its range by also providing an example of the chicken in formal dress. The combination of sweet leeks and earthy mushrooms makes the most of the thigh, and cooking the breast separately allows a control that guarantees moist flesh and crisp skin. SERVES 2

1 small chicken, about 3 lb (1.5 kg)
1 tbsp (15 mL) basic marinade (page 225)
1 tbsp (15 mL) minced onion
3 tbsp (45 mL) olive oil
½ tsp (2 mL) minced garlic
½ medium leek, white part only, chopped
1½ cups (375 mL) mixed mushrooms (such as shiitake, oyster, king oyster), trimmed and sliced

Salt and pepper
Leaves from 2 sprigs thyme
2 tbsp (30 mL) white wine
1 tbsp (15 mL) butter
¼ cup (50 mL) chicken jus (page 249)

SUGGESTED ACCOMPANIMENTS: Truffle risotto (page 111), wilted greens (page 180), roasted carrots (page 184)

Cut (or ask a butcher to cut) the chicken into pieces so that you have two boneless thighs and two suprêmes (a boneless breast with the wing drumstick attached). Massage them with the marinade and set aside in the refrigerator. Reserve the rest of the bird for another purpose.

Cook the onion in a tablespoon of the olive oil in a skillet on medium heat. When it begins to wilt, add the garlic, and a minute later stir in the leeks. As the leeks approach translucence, add the mushrooms, season lightly, and add the thyme. When the mushrooms soften, deglaze with the wine and cool in the refrigerator.

Preheat oven to 350°F (180°C).

Season the chicken on all sides. On a work surface, stretch out the thighs skin side down. Place about ½ cup (125 mL) of the mushroom-leek stuffing along the centre of each, roll the chicken around it, and bind the package closed with kitchen twine, sealing the ends as tightly as possible so the stuffing does not escape during cooking.

Heat an ovenproof nonstick skillet on medium-high and add the remaining oil and the butter. Generously season the chicken suprêmes and add them to the pan skin side down. A few minutes later add the stuffed thighs. Brown the chicken pieces on all sides—6 or 7 minutes. Then, with all chicken pieces arranged skin side up, transfer the skillet to the oven and roast, basting occasionally with the pan juices, until the chicken is well bronzed and cooked through—10 to 15 minutes. Let rest for 5 to 10 minutes, then plate the chicken with side dishes; drizzle jus around it.

Suggested wine: Pinot Noir or New World Chardonnay

Simple Roast Chicken with Root Vegetables

Whole chickens do not roast evenly. The lean breast is always done first but condemned to stay in the oven and cook some more while the muscular legs and fatty thighs catch up. Trussing a chicken—binding its limbs tightly to the carcass—only accentuates this problem. So I have long preferred to roast mine untrussed, allowing improved heat flow over the legs and thighs to shorten their cooking time, thus delivering a more uniformly succulent chicken. SERVES 2

1 tbsp (15 mL) combined finely minced sage,
    rosemary, and parsley
1 tbsp (15 mL) soft butter
1 top-quality chicken, 2½ to 3 lb (1.25 to 1.5 kg)
½ tsp (2 mL) sweet paprika
Salt
3 tbsp (45 mL) olive oil
1 sprig thyme
½ lemon, grilled until lightly charred
2 cloves garlic, smashed
½ cup (125 mL) chicken jus (optional; page 249)

ROOT VEGETABLES
2 cloves garlic, crushed
4 medium sunchokes, scrubbed and halved
4 medium variegated beets, peeled and quartered
4 small turnips, scrubbed and quartered
12 baby carrots, scrubbed and trimmed
12 fingerling potatoes, scrubbed
2 tbsp (30 mL) olive oil
Salt and pepper

Preferably 24 hours in advance, combine the herbs and butter and massage into the skin of the chicken on all sides. Sprinkle with paprika. Place on a rack and set aside in the refrigerator.

Set one rack in the lower third of the oven and another in the middle. Preheat oven to 425°F (220°C).

ROOT VEGETABLES: Combine the garlic and vegetables in a roasting pan large enough to accommodate them in a single layer. Add the oil, season, and toss well until evenly coated. Place on the lower rack of the oven.

Salt the chicken generously inside and out. In a skillet just large enough to accommodate the bird, heat the oil over medium-high heat. Brown the bird lightly on all sides. Place it breast side up on a roasting rack and carefully stuff the thyme, lemon, and garlic into the cavity. Set the rack in a roasting pan, add to it the oil from the skillet, and place in the centre of the oven.

After 15 minutes, turn the vegetables, baste the bird, and lower the heat to 350°F (180°C). After another 20 minutes, baste again. After a total roasting time of 45 minutes, test the bird for doneness—check if juices run clear from a pierced thigh or if the internal temperature of the breast has reached 160°F (70°C). Allow to rest 15 minutes before carving. Serve accompanied with the near-caramelized root vegetables and, if you choose, the chicken jus.

Substitutions: Any good root vegetables work with this dish. Whatever you select, remember to cut them up in roughly equal-sized pieces so that they will cook at the same rate.

Suggested wine: crisp Chardonnay or a light Italian red

Chicken Pot Pie with Morels

Chances are good that you remember this dish fondly from childhood. If in doubt as to why, have a go at this new version, reinvigorated with sound technique, fine ingredients, and the toothsome addition of fresh morels. SERVES 6

¼ cup (50 mL) butter
2 tbsp (15 mL) olive oil
1 cup fresh morels
½ cup (125 mL) white wine
2 lb (1 kg) boneless, skinless chicken breasts,
    ½-in (1 cm) cubes
Salt and pepper
2 shallots, minced
2 cloves garlic, crushed
1 cup (250 mL) variegated carrots, sliced
½ cup (125 mL) parsnip, sliced
½ cup (125 mL) baby turnips, halved
1 leek, sliced (white part only)

3 tbsp (45 mL) flour
2 cups (500 mL) 35% cream
3 cups (750 mL) white chicken stock (page 246), warm
2 bay leaves

TOPPING
1 sheet puff pastry, about ½ lb (250 g) total
1 tbsp (15 mL) combined minced parsley, thyme,
    rosemary, and chives
1 egg, lightly beaten

OPTIONAL
1 tsp (5 mL) gastrique (page 234)
1 tbsp (15 mL) truffle paste

Preheat oven to 375°F (190°C).

Cook the morels in 1 tbsp (15 mL) butter and ½ tbsp (7 mL) olive oil in a sauté pan over medium heat until they soften—about 5 minutes. Turn heat to high, deglaze with 2 tbsp (30 mL) of wine, and move the mushrooms to a plate. Season the chicken and add it to the pan with another tbsp (15 mL) of butter. Follow 2 minutes later with the shallots and garlic. Stirring regularly, cook the chicken to medium—about 5 to 6 minutes total. Then increase heat, deglaze with the remaining wine, and when that has all but evaporated, move the chicken to a plate. Discard the garlic, add the remaining butter, and sift in the flour. Cook for 2 minutes, then add the stock and reduced cream and whisk well. Lower to a simmer.

Meanwhile, steam the carrots and the leek until just tender. Toss the parsnip and turnips with the remaining olive oil and roast until barely tender. Divide the cubed chicken among 6 individual serving dishes (or 1 large casserole). Follow with morels and other vegetables. Whisk the sauce, correct seasonings, and, if desired, adjust acidity with gastrique and whisk in the truffle paste. Pour sauce over the chicken and vegetables to cover. To finish, sprinkle puff pastry with fresh herbs and then roll out to a thickness of about ⅛ inch (3 mm). Brush the edges of the serving dishes with egg wash, cut pastry to fit, drape it overtop, and press to seal. Brush pastry with egg wash, transfer dishes to the centre rack of the oven, and bake until the topping is crisp and bronzed—15 to 18 minutes.

Tip: If you are using dried morels in place of fresh, reserve the water used to reconstitute them, strain it, and add it along with chicken stock when preparing the velouté.

Substitutions: If you prefer dark chicken meat along with the white, simply poach (lightly) a whole 3-lb (1.5 kg) chicken for this recipe. Then strip the skin from the chicken and tear it into bite-size pieces. Strain and skim the poaching liquid and use it as the stock for your velouté. As the recipe is written above, proceed directly from sautéing the morels to preparing the roux and velouté.

Vegetables and Other Side Dishes

The straightforward simplicity with which I like to prepare vegetables is obviously a matter of taste—but it is also a reflection of the quality of the vegetables that our local artisanal farmers have worked so hard to make available over the last couple of decades. Just as one example, the asparagus that arrive each spring from David Cohlmeyer's farm, Cookstown Greens, have such a sweetly assertive purity of flavour, I simply cannot imagine working them over to turn them into a gratin or a mousseline. To me it's not just unnecessary—it's not desirable either. There are now artisanal farmers like David working all across the country. My advice is to give them your business, and to give their heritage vegetables your respect: prepare them simply and correctly and let them speak clearly for themselves.

Sautéed Chanterelles or Other Woodland Mushrooms

SERVES 4

1 tbsp (15 mL) olive oil
1 tbsp (15 mL) butter
2 tbsp (30 mL) minced onion
8 oz (225 g) wild mushrooms, trimmed, quartered
    or sliced depending on size

1 tsp (5 mL) minced garlic
Pinch each of salt and white pepper
2 tbsp (30 mL) white wine
1 tsp (5 mL) combined minced parsley, rosemary,
    and sage

Heat oil and butter in a skillet over medium-high heat. Add the onions and mushrooms, and cook, stirring frequently. When the mushrooms begin to soften, add the garlic. Season with salt and pepper. One minute later, deglaze with the wine and stir in the herbs. Correct seasonings.

Mushroom Cabbage Rolls

SERVES 4

6 cups (1.5 L) white chicken stock (page 246)
4 large Savoy cabbage leaves

Sautéed mushrooms (recipe above)
2 tsp (10 mL) fresh foie gras (optional)

Bring the chicken stock to a simmer in a large saucepan. Add the cabbage leaves and simmer gently until tender—30 to 40 minutes. Remove the leaves, pat them dry, and carefully cut out their coarse centre rib (without completely separating the two sides of the leaves).

Divide the mushrooms evenly between the four cabbage leaves, arranging them like a log down the middle. If desired, top with foie gras. Roll up the leaves, and trim the ends so that the rolls are straight and full at the ends. Place the rolls on a sheet of parchment paper in a small pan to reheat. If not using immediately, cover with plastic wrap to keep them from drying out.

Before reheating, brush lightly with stock and butter.

Crispy Spinach Greens

SERVES 4 TO 6

1 lb (450 g) prewashed spinach*
Oil for deep-frying
Salt

Heat deep-fryer to 350°F (180°C)

Drop perfectly dry spinach directly into the hot oil in small batches and use a long fork to keep the leaves as separate from each other as possible. When the leaves suddenly darken and shrivel, use a slotted spoon or a spider to remove them to a baking sheet lined with several layers of paper towels. Move the leaves around to keep them from touching each other. Salt them generously while they are still hot.

*Spinach must be absolutely dry when it is introduced to the hot oil or it will merely spit and foam and make a mess but not get crisp. Use prewashed spinach straight from the bag.

Tip: Crispy spinach goes wonderfully with nearly all fish dishes—but keep in mind that its shelf life is short, and prepare it as closely to when needed as possible.

HERBS: Parsley and sage may be prepared much the same way and used as a garnish. Do not bother with a deep-fryer, though. Simply heat 1 cup (250 mL) vegetable oil or ordinary olive oil in a small skillet to a temperature just shy of its smoking point and drop the leaves right in, one small batch at a time. When they darken and shrivel, drain on paper towels. Season very lightly, if at all.

Wilted Greens

MAKES 4 SMALL SIDE PORTIONS

1 lb (450 g) greens
1 tbsp (15 mL) minced onion
1 tbsp (15 mL) olive oil

½ tsp (2 mL) minced garlic
1 knob of butter
Salt and pepper

SWISS CHARD: For young chard, merely trim the stems where they join the leaves; with late-season chard, cut the stems completely away from the leaf. Blanch the leaves until they wilt, and then drain. Blanch the stems until tender, shock in ice water, and either chop or leave intact, depending on size. In a sauté pan, sweat the onions in oil over medium-low heat until translucent. Add the garlic, sweat a minute longer, and add the chard. Toss until heated through. Add the butter and season.

COLLARD GREENS: Blanch trimmed leaves and proceed as above.

SPINACH: Trim tough stems, omit blanching, and proceed directly to the sauté pan. Add a pinch of nutmeg along with salt and pepper.

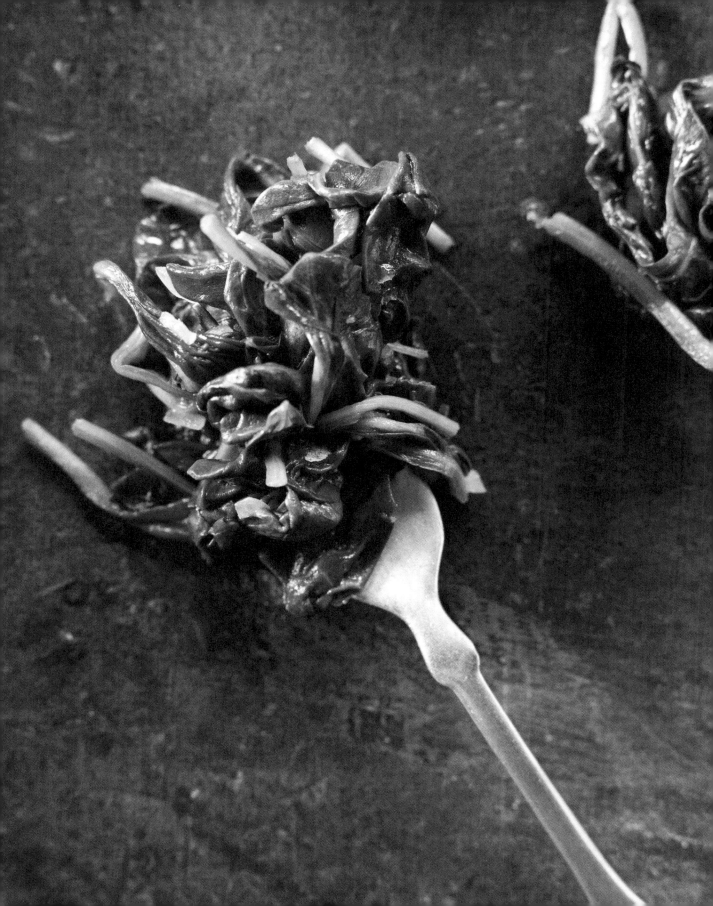

Green Asparagus

SERVES 4

1 bunch green asparagus, peeled
1 tbsp (15 mL) butter

1 tsp (5 mL) minced chives
Pinch each of salt and pepper

Blanch asparagus in a pot of vigorously boiling salted water for 90 seconds and then shock in ice water. Heat a skillet on medium-low, then add butter and asparagus. Toss until just tender and then finish with minced chives, salt, and pepper.

Grilled Green Asparagus

SERVES 4

1 bunch green asparagus, peeled
1 tsp (5 mL) fine olive oil
Pinch each of salt and pepper

Blanch asparagus in a pot of vigorously boiling salted water for 60 seconds and then shock in ice water. Heat grill, brush rack with oil, and grill asparagus for about 30 seconds per side. Remove to a serving plate. Sprinkle lightly with fine olive oil and season.

White Asparagus

SERVES 4

½ cup (125 mL) white wine
1 lemon, sliced
2 bay leaves
1 tsp (5 mL) black peppercorns
1 tsp (5 mL) salt

1 bunch white asparagus, peeled
1 tbsp (15 mL) butter
1 tsp (5 mL) minced chives
Pinch each of salt and pepper

In a large saucepan combine the wine, lemon, bay leaves, peppercorns, and salt with 2 quarts (2 L) water; bring to a boil. Blanch asparagus for 90 seconds and then shock in ice water. Heat butter in skillet on medium-low heat, add the asparagus, and sauté until just tender. Toss with the chives and season.

Roasted Root Vegetables

SERVES 4

Carrots

1 lb (450 g) heirloom carrots, scrubbed but not peeled
1 tbsp (15 mL) olive oil
1 tbsp (15 mL) butter

Pinch of ground cumin
Pinch each of salt and pepper

Preheat oven to 450°F (230°C).

Blanch the carrots for 2 to 3 minutes in boiling salted water and then shock in ice water. In the oven, heat a baking dish large enough to accommodate the carrots in a single layer. Add the carrots, oil, butter, cumin, salt, and pepper; toss to coat the carrots well. Roast, tossing every 2 minutes. Depending on their size, the carrots should be tender after 7 or 8 minutes—but watch them carefully.

Young Turnips or Sunchokes

Prepare the same way, but omit the cumin.

Fingerling Potatoes

Parboil for 6 or 7 minutes, then prepare the same way, but omit the cumin.

Roasted Beets

SERVES 4

1 lb (450 g) young variegated beets (golden, candy cane, white, red cylinder, etc.)
2 tbsp (30 mL) olive oil

3 cloves garlic, smashed
3 or 4 sprigs thyme
Salt and pepper

Preheat oven to 425°F (220°C).

Scrub beets well—do not trim, peel, or halve them or the colours will bleed. Spread a sheet of foil on a work surface. Cluster the beets in a single layer at the centre. Drizzle with olive oil. Scatter garlic and thyme overtop and season well. Create an envelope with the foil, seal it tightly, and wrap in a second layer of foil. Roast until the beets are tender—anywhere from 45 minutes for a 2-inch (5 cm) beet to nearer 2 hours for large ones (to test, protect your hand with an oven mitt or kitchen cloth and give them a squeeze through the foil).

Let the beets cool for 10 minutes before unwrapping the package. As soon as the beets have cooled enough to touch, peel them (the skin will come off like wet paper). Trim, and cut or slice as desired.

Brussels Sprouts with Bacon

SERVES 4

1 dozen Brussels sprouts
2 tbsp (30 mL) vegetable oil
¼ Spanish or Vidalia onion, sliced

¼ cup (50 mL) top-quality bacon cut into lardons
Pinch each of salt and pepper
Pecorino Romano (optional)

Preheat oven to 375°F (190°C).

Trim—and then cut a cross into—the stems of the Brussels sprouts. Blanch in boiling salted water until just tender—2 or 3 minutes—and then shock them in ice water. Drain and set aside.

Add 1 tbsp (15 mL) of the oil to a sauté pan or ovenproof skillet on low heat, and slowly caramelize the onions. After approximately 10 minutes, when they are completely wilted and beginning to brown, add the bacon. Stir frequently.

Halve the Brussels sprouts. When the bacon is beginning to brown and becoming just a little crisp around the edges, add the sprouts to the pan and sauté them briefly, allowing their water to deglaze the pan. Then add the remaining oil, season, and transfer to the oven. Roast for 30 minutes. If you choose, shave some pecorino overtop just before serving.

Fava Bean Ragout

SERVES 6

2 cups (500 mL) fresh fava beans, shucked
and peeled (see Tip)
1 red bell pepper, charred and peeled
1 yellow bell pepper, charred and peeled
1 tsp (5 mL) olive oil
1 tbsp (15 mL) butter

1 shallot (or ½ banana shallot), minced
1 small clove garlic, minced
1 tsp (5 mL) combined minced rosemary
and thyme
Pinch each of salt and pepper
1 teaspoon (5 mL) fine olive oil

Blanch the beans in a large pot of salted boiling water until just tender, then shock in ice water and reserve. Dice about a third of each bell pepper (set aside the rest for another purpose). Heat the oil and half the butter in a small saucepan. Sweat the shallots until wilted. Add the garlic and sweat a minute longer. Add the bell peppers and fava beans. Once heated through, add the herbs, season, and finish with the remaining butter. Dress each serving—or the serving bowl—with a small drizzle of olive oil.

Variation: Omit the shallot and bell peppers and instead incorporate ½ cup (125 mL) saffron pearl onions (page 197) along with ¼ cup (50 mL) chicken stock (page 246), reduce to a glaze, and finish with butter and minced chives instead of rosemary and thyme.

Tip: Favas are easier to peel after they are blanched, but their colour will be superior if you peel them beforehand. When purchasing fava beans do keep in mind that on occasion the plumpest fava pods will contain the flattest and most emaciated beans. Pop open a sample before you purchase—and even at that, always buy more than you think you will need.

Mashed Potatoes

SERVES 4

4 large Yukon Gold potatoes, peeled
1 tbsp (15 mL) salt
¼ cup (50 mL) whole milk

¼ cup (50 mL) 35% cream
¼ cup (50 mL) butter
Salt and white pepper

Bring potatoes to a boil in salted water, then reduce heat and simmer. Meanwhile, combine the milk and cream in a saucepan, scald, and set aside. When after about 25 minutes the potatoes are fork-tender and beginning to fall apart, drain them well and then pass them through a ricer or food mill. Over gentle heat, fold in the scalded milk and cream, butter, and seasonings.

Chive Mashed Potatoes

Add to base recipe:
1 bunch chives, sliced as thinly as possible (or minced)
½ cup (125 mL) crème fraîche (page 231)

Finish by folding in chives and crème fraîche. Adjust seasonings.

Ramp Mashed Potatoes

Add to base recipe:
2 bunches ramps, blanched and chopped
1 bunch chives, minced
½ cup (125 mL) crème fraîche (page 231)

Finish by folding in ramps, chives, and crème fraîche. Adjust seasonings.

Garlic Mashed Potatoes

Add to base recipe:
1 head roasted garlic (page 243), squeezed
1 bunch chives, sliced as thinly as possible (or minced)
½ cup (125 mL) crème fraîche (page 231)

Finish by folding in garlic, chives, and crème fraîche. Adjust seasonings.

Lobster Mashed Potatoes

Add to base recipe:
At least ½ cup (125 mL) cooked lobster meat (page 237), chopped
¼ cup (50 mL) buttermilk
¼ cup (50 mL) chopped chervil
¼ cup (50 mL) lobster butter (page 236)

Finish by folding in lobster meat, buttermilk, and half the chervil. Adjust seasonings. Sprinkle serving bowl or individual portions with remaining chervil and dab with lobster butter.

Perfect French Fries

SERVES 6

6 large Yukon Gold potatoes
Canola or peanut oil for deep-frying
Salt

Trim one side from the potatoes so that they sit flat and stable on the cutting board. Slice them into desired French fry size and then plunge them into ice cold water. Soak for a few hours at least—and ideally overnight—changing the water periodically.

Meanwhile, heat deep-fryer to 325°F (160°C). Dry the French fries well with a kitchen cloth and then blanch them in the hot oil until they wilt. Drain on paper towels. Raise heat on deep-fryer to 400°F (200°C). Fry the blanched French fries until bronzed and crisp. Drain and toss with lashings of salt.

Tip: Only starchy potatoes work well in the deep-fryer—and they must be fresh, not long-stored. If you cannot find large Yukon Gold potatoes, russets make a fine second choice. However, because of their thicker skins, they should be peeled. Lastly, if you do not have a deep-fryer you may simply use a deep pot and monitor the oil temperature with a candy thermometer; the oil must be at least 3 inches (8 cm) deep.

Soubise Rice Cakes

MAKES 6 RICE CAKES

1 cup (250 mL) basmati rice
1 Spanish onion, minced
5 tbsp (75 mL) soft butter
Salt
¼ cup (50 mL) grated Parmigiano-Reggiano
½ tbsp (7 mL) jalapeño paste (page 236) or minced jalapeño
1 tbsp (15 mL) clarified butter
1 tbsp (15 mL) canola or vegetable oil

Preheat oven to 350°F (180°C).

Combine rice, onion, 2 tbsp (30 mL) of the butter, and 1 tsp (5 mL) salt with 2 cups (500 mL) cold water in a lidded ovenproof saucepan. Transfer to the oven and bake until the rice is tender—about 45 minutes. Leave the pot in the oven for 15 minutes longer (leave the oven on).

Remove and let cool slightly. While the rice is still hot, pass it through a food mill fitted with the medium disc into a bowl. Add the remaining butter along with the Parmesan and jalapeño paste; mix well. Taste, and correct seasonings. Then chill to stiffen. Mould the rice mash into small pucks at least an inch (2.5 cm) thick.

Heat the clarified butter and the oil in an ovenproof nonstick skillet on medium. Fry the rice cakes until golden, then flip them, and when the second side is nearly done, transfer the pan to the oven. Bake for a further 3 to 4 minutes—but no longer, or the rice cakes will collapse.

Pearl Onions

SERVES 4

Saffron Pearl Onions

2 small pinches saffron threads
1 package (10 oz/284 g) pearl onions
2 tsp (10 mL) olive oil
Pinch each of salt and pepper

Preheat oven to 400°F (200°C).

Add 1 pinch of saffron to 1 cup (250 mL) warm water and set aside to steep. Blanch the onions in boiling salted water for 20 seconds, then shock in ice water. Drain, and then carefully trim and peel them. In a small ovenproof skillet over low to medium heat, heat the oil. Gently cook the onions, shaking the pan regularly to prevent blistering or scorching. When they become lightly bronzed, add the remaining pinch of saffron threads followed by about 2 tbsp (30 mL) of the steeped saffron tea. Shake the pan well and then transfer it to the oven. Braise the onions until they are tender and thoroughly saffron-coloured—15 to 20 minutes. Monitor carefully: shake the pan regularly, and whenever the liquid threatens to evaporate, add another 2 tbsp (30 mL) of saffron tea. Season lightly.

Roasted Pearl Onions

1 package (10 oz/284 g) pearl onions
3 sprigs thyme
3 cloves garlic, smashed
1 bay leaf
1 tbsp (15 mL) olive oil
Pinch each of salt, pepper, and granulated sugar

Preheat oven to 300°F (150°C).

Blanch, trim, and peel the onions as described above. Spread a sheet of parchment paper on top of a sheet of foil and cluster the onions at its centre. Scatter thyme, garlic, and bay leaf overtop and then drizzle with olive oil. Sprinkle lightly with salt, pepper, and sugar. Fold the package into an envelope, seal tightly, place in a baking dish, and bake for 90 minutes. Allow the package to cool slightly before opening.

Variations: Small cipollini onions benefit from an identical preparation. Yellow cooking onions (allow one per person) can also be prepared in a similar manner but require either a longer cooking time (2 to 2½ hours) or a higher temperature (375°F/190°C). You do not need to blanch larger onions before peeling them.

Tempura-Battered Onion Rings

SERVES 6

3 Spanish (or other large) onions, peeled
1 cup (250 mL) sake
1 tbsp (15 mL) + 2 tsp (10 mL) minced rosemary
2 cups (500 mL) flour
½ cup (125 mL) cornstarch

1 tsp (5 mL) baking powder
1 tsp (5 mL) salt
2 cans (each 12 oz/355 mL) cold Club Soda
Canola oil for deep-frying
Pinch each of salt and pepper

Slice the onions into ½-inch (1 cm) rings, reserving smaller rings for another purpose. Place onion rings in a bowl with the sake and 1 tbsp (15 mL) of the rosemary. Toss well, cover, and marinate overnight, tossing from time to time.

Heat deep-fryer to 375°F (190°C).

Sift flour, cornstarch, baking powder, and salt into a bowl. Add the remaining 2 tsp (10 mL) rosemary, then pour in about 19 oz (570 mL) Club Soda. Stir with a whisk—but not vigorously or too thoroughly or you will destroy the carbonation. If the batter is too thick and gluey, add more soda and stir again.

Working in batches, remove onion rings from the marinade, dredge in batter, hold above the bowl for a few moments until excess batter drips off, and then plunge into the hot oil. Deep-fry for about 3 to 4 minutes or until the onions appear brown and crisp. Drain on paper towels and season.

Tip: If you prefer a more thickly battered onion ring, dredge the marinated onions in flour before coating them in the wet batter.

Desserts

For many people dessert means cheese, but I assure you that you will find the ones we've included here to be much more refreshing. Most of them come from the menu at North 44, but they include desserts for every occasion, even small bites to pass around with coffee at the conclusion of a party. None of them is complicated, and I encourage even those who are less at ease in the sweet kitchen to give them a try.

Ice Cream

The difference in texture and flavour between homemade ice cream and even a top-quality commercial brand is as stark as that between a croissant from Poîlane or Le Nôtre and those squishy, pallid ones they peddle at your local 7-Eleven. Domestic ice-cream machines are now very affordable and easy to use. We strongly recommend that you give one a try.

MAKES ABOUT 1 QUART (1 L)

Crème Fraîche Ice Cream

2 cups (500 mL) 35% cream
6 egg yolks
½ cup (125 mL) granulated sugar
½ cup (125 mL) crème fraîche (page 231) or sour cream

Scald the cream. Whisk together the egg yolks and sugar until thick and pale. Temper the egg mixture (so that it will not curdle) by vigorously whisking in ¼ cup (50 mL) of the hot cream. Slowly add the rest of the hot cream, whisking all the while. Transfer the mixture to a saucepan and—stirring constantly, and paying special attention to the bottom of the pot—slowly bring it to a temperature of 185°F (85°C). Pour the mixture into a bowl placed inside another, larger bowl half full of ice water, and whisk vigorously to chill it. Once cooled, whisk in the crème fraîche, then cover the mixture and transfer it to the refrigerator. Once it has completely cooled, strain it through a fine-mesh sieve into an ice-cream maker, and follow the manufacturer's instructions.

Vanilla Ice Cream

1 tsp (5 mL) vanilla extract (or ½ vanilla bean, scraped)

Follow the main recipe, adding the vanilla to the cream when you first heat it, and omitting the crème fraîche.

Cinnamon Ice Cream

2 tbsp (30 mL) ground cinnamon

Follow the recipe for vanilla ice cream, but replace that flavouring with the cinnamon.

Peanut Butter Ice Cream

7 egg yolks
1 cup (250 mL) granulated sugar
2 cups (500 mL) 2% milk
2 cups (500 mL) 35% cream
¾ cup (375 mL) smooth peanut butter

Follow the instructions for crème fraîche ice cream, whisking the peanut butter into the scalded milk and cream.

Piña Colada Ice Cream

1 pineapple, peeled and cubed
1 can (13 oz/369 mL) coconut milk
½ cup (125 mL) granulated sugar
1 tbsp (15 mL) coconut rum
1 tsp (5 mL) salt

Purée all ingredients in a blender and then strain into an ice-cream maker. Follow the manufacturer's instructions.

Apple Crostata with Caramel Sauce and Sweet Crème Fraîche

In place of the customary berries or peaches, this crostata is wrapped around caramel-glazed apple—and what more do you really need? All the same, at North 44 we take it further, setting the crisp pastry shell down on a pool of rich caramel and then dressing it with thick sweetened crème fraîche, crunchy pecan praline, and a sugared apple disc. These beautiful tarts are recommended for any home cook content to risk making dessert the highlight of the meal. **MAKES 8 TARTS**

8 Granny Smith apples, peeled, cored, and diced
3 cups (500 mL) granulated sugar
2 tsp (10 mL) ground cinnamon
2 cups (500 mL) caramel sauce (page 229)
1 cup (250 mL) dry bread crumbs
Pinch of salt

1 batch pâte brisée (page 239)
1 egg, lightly beaten
1 cup (250 mL) pecan praline (page 229), chopped
  (optional)
1 batch sweet crème fraîche (page 249)
8 apple chips (optional; page 224)

Combine the diced apple with 2 cups (500 mL) of the sugar in a bowl, cover, and refrigerate overnight. Transfer the apples to a colander to drain, pressing on them lightly to expel excess liquid. Combine the apples in a bowl with the remaining sugar and the cinnamon. Add 1 cup (250 mL) of the caramel sauce, the bread crumbs, and salt and mix well.

Roll out pastry on a floured work surface to a thickness of about ⅛ inch (3 mm). Cut 8 discs from it with a 5-inch (12 cm) round cookie cutter. Mound a ball of apple mixture at the centre of each pastry disc. Brush the edges with egg wash and fold the pastry up over the filling, crimping it every inch or so. The apple must be walled in but its top should remain exposed. Transfer the tarts to a baking sheet lined with parchment paper and freeze them completely—this will ensure they retain their shape when baked.

Preheat oven to 350°F (180°C).

Transfer tarts directly from the freezer to the oven. Bake until well bronzed—about 30 minutes. Rest briefly. To serve, spread 2 tbsp (30 mL) of the remaining caramel sauce at the centre of each plate. Place the warm tart on top. If you choose, sprinkle it with chopped pecan praline, top with a quenelle of sweet crème fraîche, and finish with an apple chip.

Grasshopper Pie

Even the simplest homemade dessert is more satisfying than something purchased. If you lack time for the job, try this easy pie, which North 44 chef Sash Simpson's mother used to make at Christmas. Sash has 32 brothers and sisters—really—so if his mother could find the time, so can you. MAKES ONE 10-INCH PIE, 10 TO 12 SERVINGS

2 cups (500 mL) Oreo baking crumbs or
    pulverized chocolate wafers
½ cup (125 mL) butter, melted
½ cup (125 mL) milk
32 large marshmallows
¼ cup (50 mL) green crème de menthe
1½ cups (375 mL) 35% cream
1 tbsp (15 mL) chocolate shavings

Stir together the crumbs and butter in a bowl and then press the mixture into the bottom and sides of a 10-inch (25 cm) springform pan. In a heavy-bottomed saucepan, warm the milk and marshmallows over low heat, stirring frequently until the marshmallows are almost completely melted. Transfer the mixture to a bowl, being careful not to dislodge any burnt or brown residue from the bottom of the pot. Refrigerate until the mixture is sufficiently thickened that it mounds on its surface when poured from a spoon—about 20 minutes. Stir in the crème de menthe. In a large bowl, whip the cream until it forms stiff peaks. Fold the cream into the green marshmallow mixture and then pour the pie filling into the crust. Refrigerate until the filling sets—about 1½ hours. Sprinkle with chocolate shavings and serve.

Lemon Curd Millefeuille

This delectable dessert features crisp pastry with a refreshingly tart filling. It makes a pretty plate—especially if you dress it with the raspberry coulis. But while it appears and tastes impressively complicated, it is in fact easy and quick to prepare. MAKES 6

¾ cup (175 mL) lemon juice, strained
6 egg yolks + 1 whole egg, lightly beaten
1¼ cups (300 mL) sweetened condensed milk,
    at room temperature
1 package (16 oz/454 g) phyllo pastry
¼ cup (50 mL) butter, melted

1 tbsp (15 mL) icing sugar
1 handful fresh raspberries (optional)
1 batch raspberry coulis (optional; page 243)

CANDIED LEMON PEEL
Peel from 2 lemons, julienned
2 cups (500 mL) + 2 tbsp (30 mL) granulated sugar

In a medium saucepan, heat the lemon juice to a bare simmer. Whisk 1 tbsp (15 mL) into the beaten eggs, and then another, and then whisk all the egg mixture into the lemon juice. Heat, stirring constantly, until three bubbles have appeared on the surface. Immediately strain the mixture through a fine-mesh sieve, pushing it through with a wooden spoon. Transfer to the refrigerator. Once it has cooled, whisk in the condensed milk and refrigerate again.

Preheat oven to 350°F (180°C).

Working quickly, slice phyllo sheet into 9 2½-by-12-inch (6 by 30 cm) strips and stack them under a damp kitchen towel. Remove one strip, brush generously with some melted butter, and sprinkle with some icing sugar. Place another strip on top and dress it the same way. Repeat. Cut the three-ply package lengthwise into two equal strips. Quickly cut each of those into three rectangles about 4 inches (10 cm) long. Repeat the entire process twice, to make 18 three-ply rectangles. Spread the rectangles over a baking sheet lined with parchment paper. Place another sheet of parchment paper on top, and top with a second baking sheet to keep them flat. Bake until crisp and golden—about 12 minutes. Uncover the rectangles and let cool on the baking sheet.

CANDIED LEMON PEEL: Place the lemon peel in a small pot and cover with ice-cold water. Bring to a boil. Drain, and repeat twice. Combine 2 cups (500 mL) of the sugar with 1 cup (250 mL) water and bring to a simmer. Add the lemon peel and cook until translucent—about 10 minutes. Strain, spread the peel on a baking sheet, and let dry for 20 minutes. Sprinkle with the remaining 2 tbsp (30 mL) sugar. (The peel can be made up to a day ahead—store in sealed container.)

TO ASSEMBLE: Place one layer of pastry at the centre of each plate. Top with a layer of lemon curd piped through a pastry bag. Repeat. Top the third layer of pastry with a single dollop of curd. Scatter with candied lemon peel. If desired, garnish with a fresh raspberry or two, and finish by encircling the pastry with a drizzle of coulis.

Beignets

Alas, it's true: the Americans did not invent the doughnut, they merely thought of twisting the French _beignet_ into a fresh shape. (A bigger one, of course.) This recipe for the original produces a light, crisp, and flavourful pastry that goes brilliantly with a fine cup of coffee. And the unspeakably easy-to-prepare _dulce de leche_ is the perfect accompaniment. MAKES 20 TO 30 BEIGNETS

1 can (10 oz/300 mL) sweetened condensed milk
1 package (8 g) active dry yeast (or 20 g fresh yeast)
7 oz (200 mL) 2% milk
½ cup (125 mL) butter
1 tbsp (15 mL) granulated sugar
2 eggs
2 cups (500 mL) flour
½ tsp (2 mL) salt
Canola or vegetable oil for deep-frying
¼ cup (50 mL) granulated sugar (optional)

For the _dulce de leche_, place the unopened can of condensed milk in a heavy-bottomed saucepan, add water up to its rim, bring to a boil, and then simmer for 3 hours—really!—topping up the water periodically as it evaporates. Remove the can and allow to cool slightly before opening.

Proof the yeast according to the manufacturer's instructions. Combine the milk, butter, and 1 tbsp (15 mL) sugar in a saucepan and bring to a boil over medium heat, stirring now and then. Set aside to cool slightly. Whisk the eggs in a large bowl, and while continuing to whisk, slowly pour in the hot milk mixture until the two are completely blended. Allow to cool for a few minutes. Now begin adding the flour through a sieve, folding it in constantly with a spatula to prevent clumping. When the flour has been incorporated, fold in the salt, and then fold in the yeast. Cover with plastic wrap and let sit on the countertop for 20 minutes.

Heat deep-fryer (or oil in a deep skillet) to 350°F (180°C).

Wet your hands under cold running water and form the dough into 20 to 30 balls. Drop them directly into the deep-fryer as you form them. Jostle and roll them with tongs if necessary so that they cook evenly. Once bronzed on all sides, remove _beignets_ to drain on paper towels. If desired, sprinkle them with sugar while still hot. You may use the _dulce de leche_ as a dipping sauce—or, if you prefer, poke a hole in each _beignet_, load the _dulce de leche_ into a pastry bag, and inject it directly inside.

Variation: Instead of _dulce de leche_ use chocolate sauce (page 230).

Dark Chocolate Torte

The exceptional quality of this torte belies the utter simplicity of its preparation. The key to its airy lightness is to use the very finest quality of chocolate, but one that is well shy of bitter. If you use dark chocolate of a purity greater than 60%, the lightness will be compromised, not enhanced. MAKES ONE 10-INCH TORTE, 10 TO 12 SERVINGS

1 lb (450 g) top-quality dark chocolate (54–58% cocoa butter)
1 cup (250 mL) butter
8 whole eggs
½ cup (125 mL) granulated sugar

SUGGESTED ACCOMPANIMENTS: Whipped cream or crème fraîche ice cream (page 205), passion fruit sauce (page 239) or raspberry coulis (page 243)

Preheat oven to 300°F (150°C). Grease and flour a 10-inch (25 cm) springform pan.

Melt together the chocolate and butter in a double boiler or over a very gentle heat. Meanwhile, place the eggs in their shells in a bowl and cover them generously with hot water from the tap. Let the eggs warm for about 5 minutes. Then crack the eggs into the bowl of a stand mixer, add the sugar, and whisk on high until the volume has tripled—about 7 minutes. Transfer the melted butter and chocolate to a large bowl and fold in the whipped eggs until the mixture is smooth and uniform. Pour the batter into the prepared pan. Cover with parchment paper. Bake until the torte has doubled in size and its centre is completely set—a toothpick will come out clean—about 75 minutes. Cool slightly and serve warm.

Tip: Warm eggs aerate much more eagerly than cold ones and so create a lighter cake.

Sticky Toffee Pudding

The English rather famously love their desserts—or puddings, as they say there. This one is a classic, the definition of comfort food for any Englishman with a sweet tooth. It is quick and easy to prepare, and like a good book, hard to put down. MAKES ABOUT 10 SERVINGS

1½ cups (375 mL) chopped pitted Medjool dates
¾ cup (175 mL) chestnut purée
¼ cup (50 mL) brandy
1 tsp (5 mL) baking soda
1 cup (250 mL) granulated sugar
3 tbsp (45 mL) cool butter
2 eggs, at room temperature
1½ cups (375 mL) flour
2 tsp (10 mL) baking powder
½ tsp (2 mL) ground cinnamon

½ tsp (2 mL) ground ginger
¼ tsp (1 mL) nutmeg

SAUCE
½ lb (250 g) butter
2½ cups (625 mL) brown sugar
1½ cups (375 mL) 35% cream
1 tsp (5 mL) vanilla extract
¼ cup (50 mL) brandy

Preheat oven to 350°F (180°C). Line the bottom and sides of an 8½-inch (22 cm) springform pan with parchment paper.

Combine the dates, chestnut purée, brandy, and baking soda in a bowl. Stir in 1 cup (250 mL) boiling water. Cover and let steep for 10 minutes. Meanwhile, combine the sugar and butter in the bowl of a stand mixer and beat at low speed until combined. Add one egg, and once that is incorporated add the second. Add and incorporate the steeped date mixture. Sift together the flour, baking powder, cinnamon, ginger, and nutmeg, and add that too. Turn off the mixer and fold in any unincorporated dry components by hand. Pour the batter into the prepared pan. Bake until the centre is firm to the touch—60 to 75 minutes. Let cool slightly.

Meanwhile, make the sauce: Combine the butter, sugar, and cream in a saucepan, bring to a boil, then remove from the heat. Fold in the vanilla and brandy.

Puncture the surface of the warm cake all over with a chopstick or skewer. Pour half the sauce over the cake and let it be absorbed. Use the remaining sauce to pour over individual servings. Serve warm.

Biscotti with Cranberries and Pistachios

Biscotti are the ideal accompaniment to a bracing espresso—and as it happens, not much more difficult to make than the demitasse of coffee with which they go so nicely. The recipe that follows is in effect a formula that you can apply to innumerable flavourings. A handful of good suggestions are listed below—and your own experimentation is encouraged.
MAKES 15 TO 20 BISCOTTI

1½ cups (375 mL) granulated sugar
½ cup (125 mL) cold butter, diced
2 large eggs, at room temperature
2½ cups (625 mL) flour
1 tsp (5 mL) baking powder

½ tsp (2 mL) salt
1 cup (250 mL) dried cranberries
1 cup (250 mL) pistachios
1 egg white

Preheat oven to 325°F (160°C).

Combine the sugar and butter in the bowl of a stand mixer and mix with a paddle on low speed until pale and mildly aerated. Add one egg, and after it has been completed incorporated, add the second. Sift together the flour, baking powder, and salt and add to the mixer; mix on low speed. When it is almost completely incorporated, add the cranberries and pistachios. As soon as they are folded in, stop the mixer.

Line a baking sheet with parchment paper. Transfer the dough to the baking sheet and form it into a log about 10 inches long, 4 inches wide, and 1 inch tall (25 by 10 by 2.5 cm). Brush the surface with egg white and bake until golden brown—30 to 35 minutes. Cool the log to room temperature (but do not chill).

Lower oven to 200°F (95°C). Use a bread knife to slice the log diagonally into 15 to 20 pieces. Transfer each slice to a rack on a baking sheet. Dry in the oven until hard—15 to 20 minutes.

Variations: The humble biscotti is an exceptionally versatile vehicle for many flavourings. For orange-flavoured biscotti, replace the cranberries and pistachios with the rasped zest of 2 oranges along with 1 tbsp (15 mL) of Grand Marnier. For a chocolate version, swap ½ cup (125 mL) of the flour for an equal quantity of cocoa powder, and in place of the berries and nuts add 1 cup (250 mL) of roughly chopped dark chocolate.

Vanilla-Cardamom Cupcakes with Buttercream

These are quite simply the lightest, fluffiest, most divine cupcakes conceivable.
MAKES 12 CUPCAKES

½ cup (125 mL) cool butter, diced
1¼ cups (300 mL) granulated sugar
½ vanilla pod, scraped (or 1 tsp/5 mL vanilla extract)
2 extra-large eggs, at room temperature or warmer
1¼ cups (300 mL) cake-and-pastry flour
2 tsp (10 mL) baking powder
½ tsp (2 mL) baking soda
Pinch of salt
Seeds from 3 green cardamom pods, crushed
   (or ¼ tsp/1 mL ground green cardamom)
1¼ cups (300 mL) sour cream

BUTTERCREAM
1 cup (250 mL) granulated sugar
¼ cup (50 mL) corn syrup
4 egg whites, at room temperature or warmer
Pinch of salt
½ lb (250 g) butter, at room temperature
1 oz (30 g) white chocolate, melted
A few drops of rosewater (optional)

Preheat oven to 350° (180°C).

Combine butter and sugar in the bowl of a stand mixer and beat with a paddle on low speed until off-white and fluffy (be patient). Beat in the vanilla, and then add the eggs one at a time, blending well on low speed after each addition. Use a spatula to scrape down the sides of the bowl and ensure that nothing is left unincorporated. Sift together the flour, baking powder, baking soda, and salt. Add the crushed cardamom. Add about a quarter of this dry mix to the bowl and beat just to incorporate. Mix in about a third of the sour cream, and continue, alternating between dry and wet and finishing with the dry mix. Do not overbeat.

Line a muffin pan with paper liners and fill them with batter no more than three-quarters full. Bake until a toothpick inserted in the centre comes out clean—about 15 minutes. Cool on a rack before applying the icing.

BUTTERCREAM: In a saucepan combine the sugar, corn syrup, and 1 cup (250 mL) of warm water. Over low heat, and stirring frequently, bring to a temperature of 120°F (50°C). Place egg whites in the bowl of a stand mixer and whisk on medium speed until frothy and thick. Add a pinch of salt and then raise speed to high; slowly add the hot syrup mixture, pouring it down the sides of the bowl rather than on the whisk. Scrape down the sides of the bowl with a spatula to help incorporate the syrup. Beat in the butter and then the white chocolate—and, if you choose, the rosewater. Apply to cupcakes with a pastry bag or spatula.

Variations: For a chocolate cupcake, omit the vanilla and cardamom and exchange ¼ cup (50 mL) of the pastry flour for an equal quantity of cocoa powder. Sweet crème fraîche (page 249) also works as a superb icing for these light cupcakes in either flavour.

Basic Recipes

This section includes components of many of the preceding recipes—everything from stocks to aïolis, icings, and sauces are to be found here. The other recipes are the star attractions, but these are the

building blocks that make them turn out right. In many ways that makes it the most important section of the book. Master these basics and all the rest will fall into place handily.

Aïolis

EACH MAKES ABOUT 1½ CUPS (375 ML)

Truffle

1 egg	1 tbsp (15 mL) truffle paste	2 tbsp (30 mL) rice wine vinegar
2 tbsp (30 mL) Dijon mustard	1 cup (250 mL) vegetable oil	Salt and pepper

Whisk together the egg, mustard, and truffle paste. Continue whisking while adding the oil in a slow, steady stream. When finished, thin with vinegar to taste, then season. Keeps, refrigerated, for 3 days.

Lemon-Garlic

Omit mustard and truffle paste. Proceed as above, beginning with the egg and 1 minced clove of garlic, and finishing with lemon juice instead of vinegar.

Chili-Citrus

Omit mustard and truffle paste. Proceed as above, beginning with the egg and 1½ tbsp (23 mL) sambal oelek, and finishing with either lemon juice or vinegar.

Apple Chips

2 cups (500 mL) granulated sugar
1 Granny Smith apple

Combine sugar with ½ cup (125 mL) water and bring to a simmer. With a mandoline or very sharp knife, slice apple crosswise into a dozen-odd large, thin discs. (There is no need to core the apple.) Drop them into the simmering sugar water. As soon as they become translucent, remove to a baking sheet lined with parchment paper. Leave to dry. Will keep a couple of days in a tightly sealed container.

Asian Glaze

For pork belly

2 cloves garlic, minced
1 tbsp (15 mL) grated fresh ginger
1 tbsp (15 mL) vegetable oil
2 tbsp (30 mL) coriander seeds, toasted 3 minutes
2 tbsp (30 mL) fennel seeds, toasted 3 minutes
4 star anise, toasted 3 minutes
2 cups (500 mL) honey
1 cup (250 mL) soy sauce
1 cup (250 mL) sake
1 cup (250 mL) brown sugar
½ cup (125 mL) orange juice
2 tbsp (30 mL) rice wine vinegar
1 tsp (5 mL) sambal oelek

Gently fry the garlic and ginger in the vegetable oil 3 to 5 minutes—do not brown. Add the remaining ingredients and simmer until syrupy—about 1 hour.

For bok choi

1 cup (250 mL) hoisin sauce
1 cup (250 mL) oyster sauce
¼ cup (50 mL) rice wine vinegar
2 tbsp (30 mL) sesame oil
1 tbsp (15 mL) sambal oelek

Combine all ingredients in a saucepan, bring to a boil, then cool.

Barbecue Sauce

4 cups (1 L) ketchup
½ cup (125 mL) brown sugar
½ cup (125 mL) apple cider vinegar
¼ cup (50 mL) molasses
¼ cup (50 mL) honey
¼ cup (50 mL) Worcestershire sauce
2 tbsp (30 mL) dark rum
2 tbsp (30 mL) yellow mustard

1 tbsp (15 mL) chili powder
1 tbsp (15 mL) liquid smoke
2 tsp (10 mL) pepper
2 tsp (10 mL) garlic powder
1 tsp (5 mL) ground allspice
¼ tsp (1 mL) ground cloves
Salt

Combine all ingredients in a saucepan and simmer for 15 minutes or until desired consistency is obtained.

Basic Marinade

1 cup (250 mL) olive oil
1 tbsp (15 mL) each chopped rosemary, sage, thyme, and parsley
3 cloves garlic, chopped

Combine all ingredients and let steep for at least an hour. Marinade will keep, refrigerated, for up to a week.

Note: For any recipe that calls for "basic marinade" you may simply substitute minced fresh herbs mixed with a little olive oil. In our kitchens, we enjoy the convenience of always having this marinade on hand—and the flavour benefits from having the herbs steep in the oil.

Basic Tomato Sauce

½ medium Spanish onion, sliced
4 cloves garlic, sliced
2 tbsp (30 mL) olive oil
1 can (28 oz/796 mL) San Marzano Roma tomatoes, juice included
Leaves from 1 bunch basil
½ tsp (2 mL) cracked black pepper
Salt

In a saucepan, sweat the onions and garlic in the oil until wilted and translucent—do not brown. Add the tomatoes with their juice, half the basil, and the cracked pepper; cover and simmer 90 minutes. Pass through a food mill fitted with a medium disc and add remaining basil and salt to taste.

Braised Fruit

EACH SERVES 4

Sautéed Peaches

Preheat oven to 325°F (160°C). Heat oil and butter in an ovenproof skillet over medium heat. Add peach halves cut side down. When they begin to acquire colour—after 3 to 5 minutes—add the sugar and then deglaze with the wine. Transfer pan to the oven for 10 minutes—or until the peaches soften. Remove, and with the aid of kitchen tongs remove their skins.

Substitutions: The same method can be used with apricots or black plums. If you prefer the flavour of bourbon or an eau de vie in place of the white wine, use half the wine and spike it with 1 to 2 tbsp (15 to 30 mL) of liquor.

Riesling-Braised Apples

2 cooking apples, peeled and cored
1 tbsp (15 mL) olive oil
1 tbsp (15 mL) butter
2 tbsp (30 mL) granulated sugar
2 cups (500 mL) dry Riesling

Cut apples into 10 or 12 wedges each. Sauté for 2 to 3 minutes in oil and butter, dust with the sugar, sauté a minute longer, then add wine—which should half-cover the fruit. Cook, tossing occasionally, until wine becomes a virtual syrup and apples are just tender and lightly bronzed.

Riesling Apple Sauce

Follow the above recipe with apples cut into ¼-inch (5 mm) dice. When apples are cooked, whiz half of them in a blender, then recombine for a sauce with texture.

Riesling-Braised Quince

2 quince, peeled, cored, and diced
1 tbsp (15 mL) butter
1 tbsp (15 mL) olive oil
2 cups (500 mL) dry Riesling
1 tbsp (15 mL) granulated sugar

Sauté quince in butter and oil for 2 or 3 minutes, then add Riesling and reduce completely, by which time the quince should be fully cooked. Taste and adjust sweetness with sugar if necessary.

Braised Oxtail

2 lb (1 kg) oxtail, cut into 4 pieces
3 tbsp (45 mL) olive oil
Salt and pepper
1 Spanish onion, chopped
1 celery stalk, chopped
6 cloves garlic, smashed
1 cup (250 mL) chopped carrot
1½ Roma tomatoes, quartered
1 cup (250 mL) white wine
6 cups (1.5 L) white chicken stock (page 246)
Bouquet garni (2 bay leaves, 2 sprigs each thyme and parsley, 1 sprig rosemary)

Preheat oven to 325°F (160°C). Rub oxtail pieces lightly with some of the olive oil and season them very generously. In a Dutch oven over medium-high heat, sear them in half the remaining oil. When well browned on all sides, set them aside. Pour off oil and add remaining oil to the pan. Cook onions, with salt to help prevent browning. After a few minutes add the celery, garlic, and carrot. Cook until soft. Add the tomatoes and wine. When wine has reduced by half, return the oxtail to the pot, along with any accumulated juices. Add enough stock to cover, bring to a simmer, cover, and transfer to the oven. Oxtail will require 3 to 4 hours to become tender—remove only when the meat loses its springiness when prodded with a fork. Check periodically to make sure the meat remains submerged, and add a little stock if necessary. Add the bouquet garni when the cooking is almost complete. When the pot is removed from the oven, let it all steep together for at least 30 minutes. Remove oxtail and strip meat from the bone. Remove herbs from the braising liquid and return meat to the pot, using a fork to mash the vegetables and break apart the meat. Taste and adjust seasonings.

Variation: If instead of a rustic ragù you want one of refined appearance, do not return the oxtail to the pot. Rather, set it aside, strain the vegetables from the braising liquid and discard. Let liquid settle and skim the fat. Finely dice some onion, carrot, and celery and sauté in olive oil. Deglaze with white wine, add oxtail meat and braising liquid, and correct seasonings. Stir in butter just before serving.

Butter Sauce

½ cup (125 mL) white wine
¼ cup (50 mL) rice wine vinegar
¼ cup (50 mL) lemon juice
¼ medium Spanish onion, sliced
½ tsp (1 mL) minced jalapeño
4 slices Japanese-style pickled ginger + 1 tbsp (15 mL) of its juice
3 tbsp (45 mL) 35% cream
½ lb (250 g) butter, cubed
Salt

In a medium saucepan, combine the wine, vinegar, lemon juice, onion, jalapeño, ginger, and ginger juice. Bring to a boil, then simmer for 15 minutes. Stir in the cream and simmer for another 15 minutes. Whisk in butter piece by piece. Whiz with a hand wand or in a blender, pass through a strainer into the top of a double boiler or a clean pot, and salt to taste. Sauce is stable and can be kept warm—ideally in a double boiler. Froth with a hand wand if desired.

Candied Pistachio Praline

1 cup (250 mL) granulated sugar
Dash of lemon juice
2 tbsp (30 mL) butter
2 cups (500 mL) pistachios, toasted

Over low heat liquefy the sugar with the lemon juice and ¼ cup (50 mL) water, and then reduce until mixture attains an amber colour. Off the heat, stir in the butter, then fold in the pistachios. Spread the mixture on a baking sheet lined with parchment paper and let cool.

Variation: For pecan praline, replace the pistachios with an equal quantity of toasted pecans.

Caramel Sauce

MAKES ABOUT 1 CUP (250 ML)

1 cup (250 mL) granulated sugar
1 drop lemon juice
1 tbsp (15 mL) corn syrup
¾ cup (175 mL) 35% cream
2 tbsp (30 mL) butter
Pinch of salt

Combine sugar and ¼ cup (50 mL) water in a saucepan, add the lemon juice, and stir over low heat. As soon as the sugar has completely dissolved, add the corn syrup. When the mixture turns amber, add the cream and boil for 60 seconds. Remove from the heat and whisk in the butter and salt.

Chocolate Sauce

MAKES ABOUT 3 CUPS (750 ML)

8 oz (250 g) milk chocolate, chopped
8 oz (250 g) dark chocolate, chopped
2 cups (500 mL) 35% cream

Put chopped chocolate in a bowl.
Boil the cream, then strain it over chocolate.
Whisk together thoroughly.

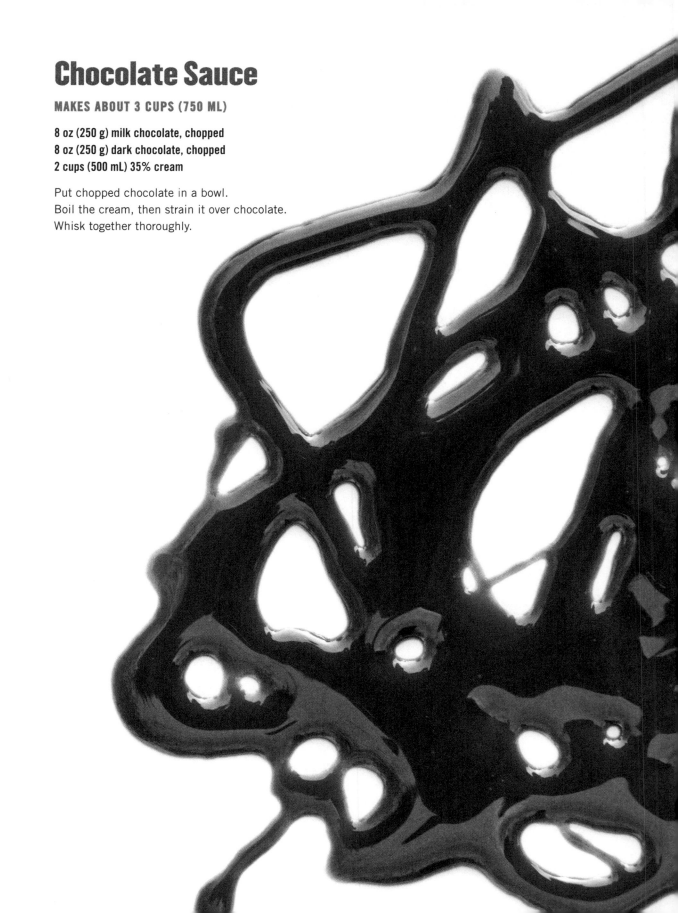

Crème Fraîche

2 cups (500 mL) 35% cream
¼ cup (50 mL) buttermilk
¼ cup (50 mL) lemon juice

Combine all ingredients in a bowl, cover, and let stand at room temperature for 24 hours. The mixture should be thick. Cover tightly and keep refrigerated for up to two weeks.

Crisp Pancetta

Preheat oven to 325°F (160°C). Place thin slices of pancetta on a baking sheet lined with parchment paper and bake until crisp—about 15 minutes.

Dry Rub

MAKES 3 CUPS (750 ML)

1 cup (250 mL) Demerara sugar
½ cup (125 mL) sweet paprika
¼ cup (50 mL) salt
¼ cup (50 mL) celery salt
¼ cup (50 mL) garlic salt
¼ cup (50 mL) onion salt

3 tbsp (45 mL) chili powder
2 tbsp (30 mL) black pepper
2 tsp (10 mL) rubbed sage
1 tsp (5 mL) dry mustard
½ tsp (2 mL) ground dried thyme
½ tsp (2 mL) cayenne pepper

Sift ingredients together into a bowl, combine well, then store in a sealed jar.

Duck Confit

6 duck legs (preferably Pekin), about 8 oz (250 g) each
Pepper and kosher salt
4 bay leaves

4 sprigs thyme
2 quarts (2 L) duck fat

Season the legs very generously on all sides with salt and pepper, then arrange them in a single layer in a snug baking dish. Add the bay leaves and thyme. Cover with plastic wrap or parchment paper and then place a second dish on top of the duck and weight it with a couple of bricks, some canned tomatoes, or some such thing. Refrigerate for 24 hours.

Preheat oven to 225°F (110°C). Transfer legs skin side down to a large nonstick skillet and render fat over low heat for 15 to 20 minutes—without flipping the legs. Meanwhile, warm the duck fat in an ovenproof saucepan or Dutch oven large enough to accommodate the legs. Add duck to the fat and transfer to the oven until the flesh begins to pull away from the bone—2 to 2½ hours. Duck can be stored—either submerged in fat or vac-packed and refrigerated—for many weeks. To finish, preheat oven to 425°F (220°C), place duck skin side down in an ovenproof skillet lined with parchment paper, and transfer to the oven until bronzed and crisp—15 to 20 minutes.

Faux Aged Balsamic

1 cup (250 mL) ordinary balsamic vinegar
¼ cup (50 mL) granulated sugar

Bring the vinegar and sugar to a simmer, stirring to dissolve the sugar, and reduce by a third to a half over low heat.

Flavoured Oils

EACH MAKES 1 CUP (250 ML)

Chili Oil

1 cup (250 mL) olive oil
1 tbsp (15 mL) chili flakes

Heat oil over medium heat, add chili, and cook for 5 minutes. Set aside to steep for 15 minutes, then strain. Keeps indefinitely if tightly sealed.

Chive Oil

1 bunch chives, blanched and shocked in ice water
1 cup (250 mL) olive oil

Dry the chives well with paper towels. Combine with the oil in a food processor and blitz. Transfer to a container, seal, and let steep overnight. Strain through a coffee filter or cheesecloth. Keeps indefinitely if tightly sealed.

Cilantro Oil

Follow recipe for chive oil, replacing chives with 1 bunch of cilantro.

Foie Gras Foam

MAKES ABOUT 2 CUPS (500 ML)

1 cup (250 mL) 2% milk
2 oz (60 g) fresh foie gras

Heat milk. Sear foie gras (see page 63). Add foie gras to milk and blitz with a hand wand or in a blender. Strain. When needed, froth milk with a cappuccino maker steam spout or other milk frother.

Fragrant Soy

1 quart (1 L) soy sauce
½ stalk lemongrass, smashed, cut into pieces
½ fresh red chili, seeded
1 tsp (5 mL) minced fresh ginger
Zest of 1 orange
Zest of 1 lime
Zest of 1 lemon
2 cups (500 mL) brown sugar

Combine soy sauce, lemongrass, chili, ginger, and citrus zests in a saucepan, bring to a boil, then simmer to reduce by half. Whisk in sugar ¼ cup (50 mL) at a time, tasting frequently until it is sweet enough for your liking—you are unlikely to require all of the sugar.

Garlic Croutons

MAKES 2 CUPS (500 ML) CROUTONS

2 cups (500 mL) bread cubes
1 cup (250 mL) butter
6 cloves garlic, smashed
1 tsp (5 mL) basic marinade (page 225)
Salt and pepper

Preheat oven to 275°F (140°C). Combine all ingredients in a roasting pan or casserole dish and bake, turning frequently, until croutons are crisp and golden—about 90 minutes.

Gastrique

MAKES ¾ CUP (175 ML)

1 cup (250 mL) white wine
½ cup (125 mL) red wine vinegar
2 shallots, sliced
2 bay leaves
2 tsp (10 mL) kosher salt
1 tsp (5 mL) granulated sugar
1 tsp (5 mL) peppercorns

Combine all ingredients, bring to a boil, then simmer gently to reduce by half. Strain and cool. Keeps indefinitely in the refrigerator.

Gnocchi

5 medium Yukon Gold potatoes, about 2 lb (1 kg) total, scrubbed
1 tbsp (15 mL) salt
Pinch each of white pepper and nutmeg
¼ cup (50 mL) grated Parmigiano-Reggiano
1 tbsp (15 mL) clarified butter
1 small clove garlic, minced
1 egg, lightly beaten
½ cup + 1 tbsp (140 mL) flour

Preheat oven to 375°F (190°C). Roast potatoes until cooked through—50 to 60 minutes—then cut them open halfway, squeeze to open slightly, and return to the oven for a further 10 minutes to drive out steam. Allow to cool briefly, then scoop out insides and pass through a ricer into a bowl. Add salt, pepper, nutmeg, Parmesan, butter, garlic, and egg. Mix well, lifting the mixture and then letting it fall through your fingers so that is aerated rather than compressed. Add a third of the flour and mix again in the same manner. Repeat until all the flour is incorporated. Then press the mixture together lightly. It should be just barely tacky to the touch—if it is sticky, incorporate a little more flour. Set dough aside to rest for a few minutes. Flour a work surface. Working in batches, roll dough into a log about ¾ inch (2 cm) in diameter. Flour a knife, trim end of log at an angle, and—maintaining that angle—cut roll into equal pieces of about 1 inch (2.5 cm). Transfer gnocchi to a lightly floured baking sheet.

Bring a large pot of salted water to a vigorous boil. Add gnocchi, and stir very gently to prevent sticking. As they float to the surface—after about 3 minutes—remove them with a slotted spoon to a lightly oiled baking sheet to cool.

The gnocchi can be used at once or kept covered in the refrigerator for up to 3 days. Otherwise, freeze them.

Variations: For jalapeño gnocchi, add 1 tsp (5 mL) jalapeño paste to the above recipe. For truffled gnocchi, add 1 tbsp (15 mL) truffle paste.

Herb Tapenade

MAKES ABOUT 1 CUP (250 ML)

Leaves from ¼ bunch thyme, chopped
Leaves from ¼ bunch sage, chopped
Leaves from ¼ bunch oregano, chopped
Leaves from ¼ bunch Italian parsley, chopped
2 cloves garlic, minced
½ cup (125 mL) olive oil
3 tbsp (45 mL) red wine vinegar
Salt and pepper

Combine all ingredients; adjust seasoning.

Hollandaise

MAKES ABOUT 1½ CUPS (375 ML)

2 egg yolks, at room temperature
2 tbsp (30 mL) gastrique (page 234)
Salt and pepper
1 cup (250 mL) warm clarified butter
A few drops each Tabasco and Worcestershire sauce, and a few drops of lemon juice

Whisk yolks and gastrique together in a bowl until frothy and pale yellow; season lightly. Place the bowl on top of a pot of barely simmering water. Continue to whisk until the egg mixture thickens—but lift the bowl off the steam now and then so the eggs do not overcook and clump. When the whisk begins to leave lingering streaks in the mixture, add the warm clarified butter in a slow, steady stream while whisking continuously. When all the butter has been incorporated, add the Tabasco and Worcestershire. Taste and adjust seasonings. Keep warm.

Note: A conventional hollandaise draws its acidity exclusively from lemon juice; we find our version to be more flavourful.

Jalapeño Paste

1 tbsp (15 mL) chopped jalapeño
1 tbsp (15 mL) olive oil

Combine pepper and oil in the bowl of a mini food processor and blitz until smooth. Alternatively, pulverize the pepper with a mortar and pestle, then add oil and combine.

Lobster Butter

MAKES ABOUT 3 CUPS (750 ML)

1 shallot, minced
1 tsp (5 mL) olive oil
1 tsp (5 mL) butter
½ tsp (2 mL) minced thyme
5 oz (150 g) lobster meat, cooked and cubed
¼ cup (50 mL) brandy
1 lb (450 g) butter, at room temperature
Salt and pepper
One squeeze lemon juice
Cooked lobster roe (optional)

Sweat the shallot in oil and 1 tsp (5 mL) butter without browning it. Add the thyme, lobster, and brandy. Allow alcohol to evaporate, then remove from heat and let cool. Transfer to a food processor along with the pound of butter. Pulse several times to combine. Season with salt and pepper, add lemon juice and, if desired, the roe, and pulse once more. Keep refrigerated.

Maple-Whisky Glaze

MAKES ¾ CUP (175 ML)

1 cup (250 mL) maple syrup
½ cup (125 mL) Jack Daniel's
1 tbsp (15 mL) butter
1 tsp (5 mL) chili flakes

Combine syrup and bourbon, bring to a boil, then simmer until reduced by half. Stir in butter and chili flakes. Keeps indefinitely.

Oven-Dried Tomatoes

Any vine-ripened tomato will do. Preheat oven to 275°F (140°C). Halve tomatoes, remove seeds, and spread cut side up on a baking sheet lined with parchment paper. Sprinkle with a little minced rosemary, thyme, and sage. Scatter basil leaves overtop. Drizzle with olive oil, season with salt and pepper, and bake until dry—at least 2 hours.

Par-Cooked Lobster

½ cup (125 mL) white vinegar
1 live lobster, about 1½ lb (750 g)

Bring 8 quarts (8 L) cold water to a boil in a pot large enough to accommodate the lobster. Add vinegar and remove from the heat. Add lobster, cover, and 2 minutes later remove with a pair of tongs. With a kitchen cloth, twist off its claws and return them to the pot for an additional 5 minutes. Detach the tail from the body. Twist off the tail fan, insert a thumb, and push out the lobster meat. Remove knuckles from claws. Pull down the pincer and move it from side to side. It should detach with the cartilage attached, leaving the claw intact. Crack the claw shell and remove claw meat. Cut knuckles with kitchen shears and remove knuckle meat. Refrigerate the lobster meat until needed.

Note: If preparing more than one lobster, add sufficient water—and ½ cup vinegar for every 8 quarts water—to ensure that all lobsters are fully submerged as they steep.

For fully cooked lobster, plunge lobsters head first into a pot of court bouillon—or for the quick version, vinegar-spiked water as described. Cover and simmer for about 10 minutes for a 1½-lb (750 g) lobster to about 14 minutes for a 2½-lb (1.1 kg) lobster. Shell as described above.

Passion Fruit Sauce

4 passion fruit
¼ cup (50 mL) granulated sugar

Scrape seeds, pulp, and all pink threads from the passion fruit into a saucepan. Set aside about 2 tbsp (30 mL) seeds. Add the sugar and enough water to lubricate—about ¼ cup (50 mL). Bring to a boil, stirring, and then immediately remove from the heat. Strain. Add reserved seeds for colour. Chill until needed.

Pasta Dough

MAKES ABOUT 1 LB (450 G), ENOUGH FOR 4 MAIN-COURSE SERVINGS

1½ cups (375 mL) flour
3 eggs
1 tbsp (15 mL) salt

Sift flour into the bowl of an electric mixer fitted with a dough hook. Add the eggs, turn on the mixer at low speed, and add the salt. When the dough clumps together in a ball, turn off the mixer. The dough should be only vaguely tacky. If it is sticky to the touch, incorporate a little more flour. On a floured work surface, kneed the dough quickly for 2 or 3 minutes. Cover in plastic wrap and set aside to rest in the refrigerator for at least 30 minutes. Dust the dough with flour again before passing it through a pasta rolling machine. Add more flour if pasta sticks to the rollers (pay special attention to this in summer, when humidity is at its highest). After rolling the dough, let it rest again at room temperature for 30 minutes before using.

Pâte Brisée

2 cups (500 mL) cake-and-pastry flour, sifted
Generous pinch of salt
½ lb (250 g) butter, cubed and frozen
1 tbsp (15 mL) cider vinegar

Combine flour and salt in the bowl of a stand mixer fitted with a paddle. Turn to medium-low speed and add the butter. Mix until butter is well dispersed but still slightly clumpy. Add vinegar and ¼ cup (50 mL) water and continue to mix. Add up to—but not more than—another ¼ cup (50 mL) water to help dough to ball up. Do not overmix or the pastry will be tough. Wrap dough in plastic wrap and let rest in refrigerator for 2 hours before rolling out.

Pear and Endive Salad

2 Belgian endives, trimmed, cut diagonally into strips
1 pear, halved, cored, and thinly sliced crosswise
¼ small red onion, very thinly sliced
Sherry-shallot or lemon-garlic vinaigrette (page 250) to taste

Shortly before serving, combine ingredients, dress lightly, and toss.

Pear-Vanilla Chutney

MAKES 2 CUPS (500 ML)

½ lb (250 g) ripe pears, peeled, cored, diced
2 tbsp (30 mL) granulated sugar
¼ cup (50 mL) red wine vinegar
½ tsp (2 mL) vanilla extract
Salt

Sauté the pears with the sugar until caramelized and golden brown. Deglaze with the vinegar, then stir in the vanilla. Reduce until the liquid becomes a syrup, then cool and purée. Add salt to taste. Chutney keeps, covered and refrigerated, for up to 2 weeks or, canned and processed, up to a year.

Pickled Pears

4 cups (1 L) granulated sugar
2 cups (500 mL) apple cider vinegar
2 sticks cinnamon

1 tbsp (15 mL) ground cloves
½ medium knob of ginger, sliced
40 to 50 baby pears

In a large saucepan combine the sugar, vinegar, cinnamon, cloves, ginger, and 2 cups (500 mL) cold water. Bring to a boil, then simmer for 5 minutes, stirring to dissolve the sugar. Add the pears and simmer until tender, then cool, submerged in their liquid. Pears keep, covered and refrigerated, for up to 2 weeks or, canned and processed, up to a year.

Port Jelly

MAKES ABOUT 1 CUP (250 ML)

2 leaves of gelatin
1 cup (250 mL) port
½ cup (125 mL) granulated sugar

In a small saucepan, soak gelatin in port for 1 hour. Remove leaves, squeeze out port, and reserve. Bring port to a boil, add sugar, reduce to a simmer, and stir to dissolve the sugar. Add the gelatin and stir to dissolve. Pour into desired mould and chill.

Quick Puff Pastry

3½ cups (450 g) flour
1 lb (450 g) cold butter, cubed
1 tsp (5 mL) salt

Sift the flour into the bowl of a stand mixer with a dough hook attached. Add butter and work in slowly but not completely—the butter should be well dispersed but still visible in lumps. Meanwhile, dissolve the salt in ¾ cup (175 mL) cold water, then add to the flour and butter. Do not overwork. Transfer dough to a flour-dusted work surface, shape into a square, and let rest for 10 minutes. Roll dough out into a rectangle with a thickness of about ½ inch (1 cm). Dust the dough with flour, and then, working lengthwise, fold it into thirds like a letter so that the new rectangle is three layers deep. Dust it with flour, roll out again into a rectangle ½ inch (1 cm) thick, dust, and fold. Repeat the process three more times. Wrap the dough in plastic wrap and allow it to rest in the refrigerator for 45 minutes before using.

Raspberry Coulis

MAKES ABOUT 1 CUP (250 ML)

1 pint raspberries
¼ cup (50 mL) granulated sugar

Heat berries and sugar in a saucepan until the sugar dissolves, then purée and strain through a fine-mesh strainer.

Roasted Garlic

Preheat oven to 350°F (180°C). Place whole heads of garlic on a sheet of foil. Drizzle with olive oil and 1 tbsp (15 mL) water per head. Seal the foil package, place on a baking sheet, and roast until soft—about 1 hour.

Rouille

MAKES ABOUT 1½ CUPS (375 ML)

1 cup (250 mL) diced peeled potato, steamed
1 cup (250 mL) saffron-infused fish stock (page 246)
1 tbsp (15 mL) olive oil
1 tsp (5 mL) minced garlic
½ oil-preserved red chili, minced
3 oz (90 g) salt-cured foie gras or foie gras mousse (optional)
Pinch each of salt and pepper

Combine potato, half the stock, the olive oil, garlic, chili, and optional foie gras in a blender and whiz until smooth. Adjust texture with more fish stock if necessary. Adjust seasonings.

Sesame Crust

Grated zest of 1 lemon
Grated zest of 1 lime
Grated zest of 1 orange
3-in (8 cm) piece horseradish, grated
¼ cup (50 mL) white sesame seeds, toasted

Preheat oven to 250°F (120°C). Spread the zests and horseradish over a baking sheet lined with parchment paper. Bake until dry—about 30 minutes. Combine with sesame seeds.

Simple Syrup

Mix together equal volumes of water and sugar. Heat to dissolve the sugar, and then cool.

Soffritto

Italian Soffritto

1 cup (250 mL) minced red or white onion
½ cup (125 mL) minced celery
¼ cup (50 mL) minced fennel
¼ cup (50 mL) minced carrot
¼ cup (50 mL) minced garlic
½ cup (125 mL) olive oil

Combine the vegetables and garlic in a saucepan, add the oil, and cook over medium heat, stirring often, until vegetables are completely wilted.

Spanish Sofrito

1 red bell pepper, roasted, peeled, and chopped
2 scallions, minced
3 cloves garlic, roasted and chopped
6 anchovy fillets, minced
2 tbsp (30 mL) minced parsley
Zest of ½ lemon, minced
1 tbsp (15 mL) sherry vinegar
½ tsp (2 mL) sambal oelek

Combine all ingredients. Store in refrigerator.

Stocks and Jus

Court Bouillon

MAKES ABOUT 2 QUARTS (2 L)

2 cups (500 mL) white wine vinegar
½ large white onion, sliced
2 bay leaves
½ lemon, sliced
6 stems parsley without leaves (or 3 sprigs with leaves)
1 tbsp (15 mL) kosher salt
1 tbsp (15 mL) black peppercorns

Combine all ingredients with 2 quarts (2 L) cold water and simmer for 30 minutes.

For cooking octopus, substitute an equal quantity of red wine vinegar for the white wine vinegar.

Fish Stock

MAKES ABOUT 2 QUARTS (2 L)

2 lb (1 kg) white fish bones (such as halibut, sole, turbot, flounder), rinsed and chopped
½ Spanish onion, sliced
1 small leek, white part only, sliced
16 parsley stems
3 bay leaves
12 peppercorns
1 lemon, sliced
1 cup (250 mL) white wine
2 tbsp (30 mL) kosher salt

Combine all ingredients in a heavy-bottomed stock pot (not aluminum). Add 2 quarts (2 L) cold water, bring to a boil, and then simmer for an hour or so, skimming scum from the surface as it rises. Strain.

Veal, Beef, Pork, or White Chicken Stock

MAKES ABOUT 12 QUARTS (12 L)

10 lb (4.5 kg) veal, beef, pork, or chicken bones, cut into pieces and well rinsed
3 medium Spanish onions, very coarsely chopped
2 large carrots, very coarsely chopped
½ bunch celery, very coarsely chopped
½ bunch thyme
½ bunch parsley without leaves (or ¼ bunch with leaves)
4 bay leaves
1 tbsp (15 mL) black peppercorns

In a stockpot cover bones generously with cold water—about 15 quarts (15 L). Bring to a boil, reduce heat to a simmer, and skim the scum from the surface. When that is gone, add the remaining ingredients. Simmer, uncovered, for at least 3 hours—and up to overnight. Continue to skim scum as it rises and replenish water as needed. Strain stock, chill, then skim fat from the surface. Keeps for about 1 week in the fridge and about 6 months in the freezer.

Variation: For dark chicken stock, use roasted bones. To make vegetable stock, simply omit the bones; skimming scum and fat will be unnecessary.

Note: Stock is an invaluable commodity, and it's convenient to keep it on hand in the freezer. If the quantity above seems too large for your needs, use the reduced quantities in the following recipe.

Rabbit or Duck Stock

MAKES ABOUT 3 QUARTS (3 L)

3 lb (1.5 kg) rabbit or duck bones, chopped and rinsed
1 medium Spanish onion, very coarsely chopped
1 medium carrot, very coarsely chopped
3 celery stalks, very coarsely chopped
3 sprigs thyme
6 stems parsley without leaves (or 3 sprigs with leaves)
2 bay leaves
1 tsp (5 mL) black peppercorns

In a Dutch oven generously cover bones with cold water—about 4 quarts (4 L). Follow directions for beef, veal, pork, or white chicken stock above.

Veal Jus

MAKES ABOUT 5 CUPS (1.25 L)

10 lb (4.5 kg) veal bones, cut into pieces and well rinsed
3 medium Spanish onions, very coarsely chopped
2 medium carrots, very coarsely chopped
½ bunch celery, very coarsely chopped
½ bunch parsley without leaves (or ¼ bunch with leaves)
1 sprig each rosemary and sage
3 Roma tomatoes, halved
3 cups (750 mL) red wine
10 quarts (10 L) veal stock

Preheat oven to 450°F (230°C). Roast bones, turning them from time to time, until golden brown. Pour off fat into a large stock pot. Add chopped vegetables and sauté until lightly browned. Add the veal bones, parsley, rosemary, sage, and tomatoes. Deglaze roasting pan with 1 cup (250 mL) red wine and then add that to the stock pot. Reduce over medium-high heat to almost nothing, then add another cup of wine. Repeat. When the wine is reduced to nearly nothing, add 1 quart (1 L) of the veal stock. Reduce by half, then add another quart. Repeat until all the stock has been incorporated. Strain the jus, chill, and skim the fat.

Chicken, Duck, Rabbit, or Pork Jus

MAKES 2 CUPS (500 ML)

3 lb (1.5 kg) chicken, duck, rabbit, or pork bones, cut into pieces and rinsed
1 cup (250 mL) white wine
2 quarts (2 L) chicken, duck, rabbit, or pork stock (pages 246 and 247)
1 sprig each thyme and parsley
1 small sprig sage
Salt and pepper

Preheat oven to 450°F (230°C). Roast bones, turning them from time to time, until golden brown. Pour off fat. Deglaze roasting pan with wine. Transfer to a large saucepan and boil over medium heat. When wine has almost completely evaporated, add 1 cup (250 mL) of the stock. Reduce to nearly nothing, and repeat again and again. In the final 30 minutes or so add the herbs. When all the stock has been incorporated, strain and adjust seasonings.

Sweet Crème Fraîche

MAKES ABOUT 2 CUPS (500 ML)

2 cups (500 mL) 35% cream
¼ cup (50 mL) sour cream
1/2 tbsp (7 mL) granulated sugar
½ tbsp (7 mL) lemon juice

Combine half the cream with the sour cream, sugar, and lemon juice and whisk well. Cover and leave to stand on the counter overnight. Transfer mixture to a sieve lined with cheesecloth and drain until thick—about 2 hours. Whip the remaining cream until it forms stiff peaks. Gently but thoroughly fold the thickened crème fraîche into the whipped cream.

Tomato Concassé

About 4 Roma tomatoes yields 1 cup (250 mL) concassé. Blanch Roma tomatoes and shock in ice water. Peel and quarter. Remove tops, seeds, and pulp. Cut flesh into fine dice or diamond shape.

Tomato Water

20 ripe tomatoes
1 tbsp (15 mL) kosher salt

Purée tomatoes with the salt in a food processor. Transfer to a large plastic strainer or colander lined with a very large coffee filter or multiple layers of cheesecloth. Place raised over a bowl that will catch the dripping juices without contact. Leave to sit overnight. Then refrigerate.

Vinaigrettes and Other Dressings

Chili-Citrus Dressing

MAKES ABOUT 2 CUPS (500 ML)

Juice of 2 lemons
¾ cup (175 mL) vegetable oil
½ cup (125 mL) light soy sauce
3 tbsp (45 mL) sambal oelek

1½ tbsp (23 mL) grated fresh ginger
½ tbsp (7 mL) sesame oil
Salt and pepper

Whisk all ingredients together. Allow to steep for 45 minutes. Strain through a fine-mesh sieve.

Lemon-Garlic Vinaigrette

MAKES ABOUT 2 CUPS (500 ML)

Juice of 1 lemon
2 cups (500 mL) olive oil
1 cup (250 mL) granulated sugar
¼ cup (50 mL) minced garlic
Salt and pepper

Whisk all ingredients together. Adjust seasonings.

Maple-Walnut Vinaigrette

MAKES ABOUT 1 CUP (250 ML)

6 tbsp (90 mL) maple syrup
1/3 cup (75 mL) olive oil
¼ cup (50 mL) champagne vinegar
3 tbsp (45 mL) walnut oil
Pinch each of salt and pepper

Whisk all ingredients together. Adjust seasonings.

Sherry-Shallot Vinaigrette

MAKES ABOUT 1 CUP (250 ML)

1/3 cup (75 mL) dry sherry
1 shallot, minced
¼ cup (50 mL) sherry vinegar
2 tbsp (30 mL) Dijon mustard
1/3 cup (75 mL) olive oil
Salt and pepper

Heat the sherry and then light it to burn off the alcohol. Refrigerate until cool. Combine shallot, vinegar, and mustard. Whisk in chilled sherry and then the olive oil. Taste, and adjust seasonings.

Crème Fraîche Dressing

MAKES ABOUT 1 CUP (250 ML)

1 scallion, minced
1 clove garlic, minced
Leaves from 4 sprigs parsley, finely chopped
1 cup (250 mL) crème fraîche (page 231)
2 tbsp (30 mL) buttermilk
½ tbsp (7 mL) cider vinegar
1 tsp (5 mL) Dijon mustard
Salt and pepper

Whisk all ingredients together. Taste, and adjust seasoning.

Yuzu Dressing

MAKES ABOUT 1 CUP (250 ML)

1 cup (250 mL) soy sauce
1 clove garlic, smashed
1-in (2.5 cm) knob ginger, peeled and sliced
½ sheet kombu seaweed
1 tbsp (15 mL) mirin
6 tbsp (90 mL) sesame oil
3 tbsp (45 mL) olive oil
1 tbsp (15 mL) yuzu juice

Combine soy sauce, garlic, ginger, and kombu in a saucepan and bring to a boil. Add mirin, then reduce heat and simmer until syrupy. Blitz with a hand wand or in a blender, then strain and cool. Add sesame and olive oils and yuzu juice, and whisk or shake vigorously to combine.

Whipped Butter

1 lb (450 g) butter, at room temperature
3 ice cubes

Place butter in the bowl of a stand mixer fitted with a paddle. Blend until creamy. Add ice cubes and blend until melted and incorporated completely. Keep refrigerated.

Acknowledgments

In many ways this book reflects what I have learned over an entire career, and because of that, when it comes to thanking people for their contributions to it (intentional or not), I must start at the beginning. So I will begin by expressing a debt of gratitude to Joseph Vonlanthan, who gave me my start in the business, and that done, devoted much time to make sure I went about it right. Moving on, I must next thank Peter Shilling, the food and beverage manager at the Sutton Place, who, one December back when I was still just a kid, appointed me executive sous-chef at the hotel, and two months later made me executive chef of the entire hotel—at age twenty-four, the youngest chef to hold that position in the country. And Mr. and Mrs. Guenther Abromeit (of Lehndorff Corp., which then controlled Sutton Place) were always a great support.

There were others during those early years whom I never worked for but who were nonetheless an inspiration to me. George Minden and his Windsor Arms Hotel helped open my eyes to what was possible to accomplish in Toronto. Windsor Arms alumnus David Barette displayed it again with Fenton's on Gloucester Street. Next I must express gratitude to Franco Prevedello, who gave me my first big leg-up in the business by putting Pronto up for sale—and to the Royal Bank of Canada, which provided the financing that allowed me to buy a piece of it, as well as every business venture of mine that followed.

That brings me to the present, and the sensational team that executes my culinary vision across three restaurants, a catering business, and my grocery and fine food emporium, McEwan. At the top of the list come my executive chefs: Drew Ellerby at One, Brooke McDougall at Bymark, Ivana Raca at McEwan, and Sash Simpson at North 44 (please note, kids, this list is alphabetical and nothing more). Each of them contributed a significant number of fine recipes to this book. So did Emili Chytil, Andrew Halitsky, and Tony Accettola. I am also grateful to Minh Chan Ly, the ever-obliging anchor of my prep kitchen since 1986.

My chefs could not do their jobs as well as they do without the exceptional support of my management team: thank you Alyssa Baksh, Tiffany Smith Diggins, Tim Salmon, Darlien Scott, and Elaine Viterbo (yes, alphabetical again).

Moving from our food to the book itself, I want to thank Andrea Magyar at Penguin Group (Canada) for coming to me with both the idea and the encouragement necessary to make the project happen. I also want to thank Penguin's art director, Mary Opper, and the production team on the project, including Chrystal Kocher, Shaun Oakey, David Ross, and Janette Thompson. I should thank Jacob Richler for testing and writing all the recipes, and by the looks of him, eating them all too. And returning to my chefs, I must single out Drew Ellerby for preparing all the dishes for the photography team almost as nicely as I could have done. That team was headed most capably by food stylist Ruth Gangbar and prop stylist Laura Branson. The splendid food photography was executed by James Tse. Rob Fiocca also contributed a handful of photographs, as did Blaire Locke. The cover shot is the work of Nikki Leigh McKean.

In closing, I want to thank my television production team at General Purpose Pictures—and especially producers Scott McNeil and Josie Crimi—who oversaw production of this book from start to finish. Lastly and most importantly I must thank my wife, Roxanne, who stood by graciously and supportively once again as I focused possibly a little too much on yet another new project.

Index

Photo Credits

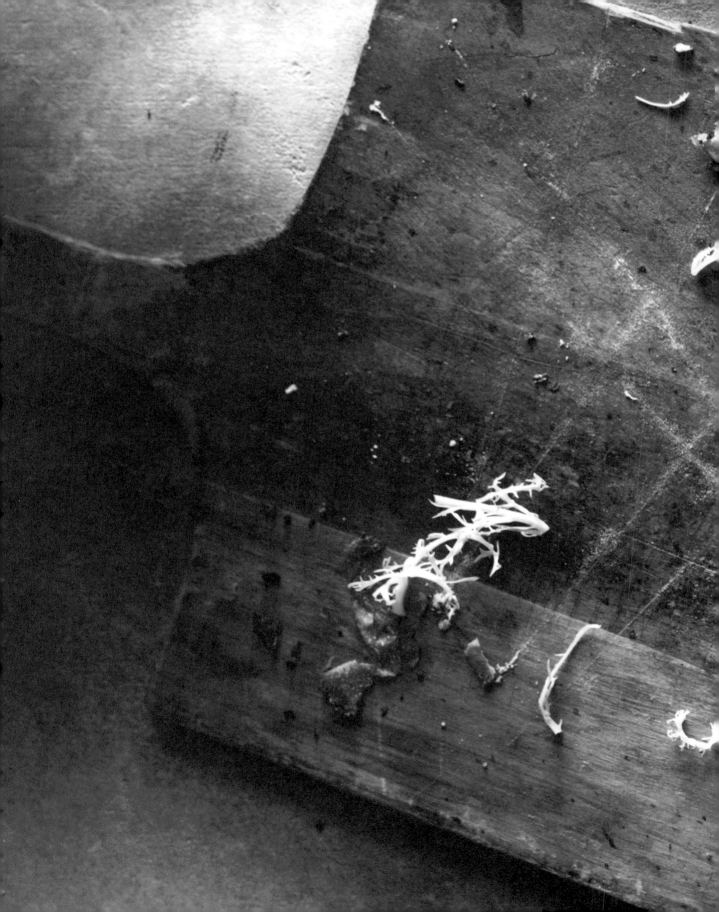